AF291426

Lucien Young is a comedy writer who has worked on various TV programmes, including BBC Three's *Siblings* and *Murder in Successville*. He was born in Newcastle in 1988 and read English at the University of Cambridge, where he was a member of the world-famous Footlights Club. His previous books include *Alice in Brexitland*, *Trump's Christmas Carol*, *The Secret Diary of Jeremy Corbyn*, and *The Secret Diary of Boris Johnson Aged 13 ¼*.

Not The Secret Diary of NIGEL FARAGE

Aged 61 3/4

Lucien Young

Harper North

HarperNorth
Windmill Green
24 Mount Street
Manchester M2 3NX

A division of
HarperCollins*Publishers*
1 London Bridge Street
London SE1 9GF

www.harpercollins.co.uk

HarperCollins*Publishers*
Macken House, 39/40 Mayor Street Upper
Dublin 1, D01 C9W8, Ireland

First published by HarperCollins*Publishers* Ltd 2026

1 3 5 7 9 10 8 6 4 2

Copyright © Lucien Young 2026
All illustrations © Quinton Winter 2026

Lucien Young asserts the moral right to be identified as
the author of this work

A catalogue record of this book is available
from the British Library

HB ISBN 978-0-00-882462-4

Printed and bound in the UK using 100% renewable electricity
at CPI Group (UK) Ltd

*To Benson & Hedges, without whom this book
would not have been written.*

*And to the nation's brewers, without whom this book
would have been written much quicker.*

'Patriotism is your conviction that this country is superior to all others because you were born in it'

George Bernard Shaw

'The past is never dead. It's not even past'

William Faulkner

'Reform has sensible positions on immigration and inheritance tax, so I stand with Nigel Farage'

Bonnie Blue

BREXIT PARTY
UKIP
Love from Enoch x

Dear reader,

Yes, it's me. Nigel Farage – duke of UKIP, baron of the Brexit Party, ruler of Reform. And, if polls are to be believed, your next prime minister. From YouGov to Ipsos, every reputable firm has my party streets ahead. While I welcome these polls (unlike their European homophone), I'm far from complacent. A week, they say, is a long time in politics, and election campaigns are an eternity. If I'm to stand grinning outside No 10, toasting the nation with a patriotic pint, I need to be prepared. I must navigate the minefield of British politics with the grace of a ballerina. Or, rather, a ballerino. A straight ballerino. Which brings us to this diary…

You may be wondering why I – a man of action rather than letters – have decided to don my reading glasses, pour a Macallan and scribble thoughts into a leather-bound notebook (passport-blue, naturally). Perhaps you're hoping

I'll bare my soul, unburden my breast, air my deepest, darkest secrets. If so, you're barking up the wrong tree. I don't do introspection; as far as I'm concerned, feelings are for women and contestants on *RuPaul's Drag Race*. No, I'm just a normal bloke who loves cricket, Clarkson and the occasional beer (that occasion being several times a day).

However, as prospective first lord of the Treasury, I feel a duty to record my rise to power. If I'm to govern this sceptred isle, there should be something for future historians to pore over. Proper historians, though – the kind who wear tweeds and tortoiseshell glasses, not the kind who bang on about colonialism on Channel 4. David Starkey, rather than David Olusoga. I don't want some hippie to write a thesis on my 'problematic attitude' towards the asexual community. But I digress.

Over the following pages, I plan to employ my trademark bluntness. I'll take you behind the scenes, illuminating the day-to-day life of a political rock star. You'll learn the ins and outs, the ups and downs, the nitty and the gritty. You'll see sides of me you never imagined – perhaps more than you'd like to see! After all, I contain multitudes: lover and fighter, hero and scoundrel, respected statesman and TikTok power user.

Most importantly, this diary will capture my struggle to bring Britain back from the brink. For more than three decades, I have defended Albion, opposing the forces that benight Blighty. I dream of a country free from woke lunacy and egghead expertise: free from sneering septum-ringed brats with rainbow hair, deranged social engineers who invent a new gender every day, and PC PCs who lock you up just for being English; free from anything that might discomfort or annoy our people – the right sort of people.

In other words, a return to the 1930s. Or, at the very least, the mid-'80s. Isn't that what we all want? (I'm assuming the reader is white, male, affluent and aged between 60 and dead.) I speak of Little England – a land of Bovril, Elgar and Morris Minors; of Victoria sponge, privet hedges and proper posties; of church raffles and street parties festooned with bunting. A place where mum, dad and two-point-four kids can gather round the goggle-box to watch grateful natives put on a display for the king, and where every soul is middle-aged, middle-class and middle-brow.

But before we return to those halcyon days, I need to get elected. How will I go about it? Let's find out together…

Nigel Farage MP

Clacton-on-Sea (wink)

202—

1.

REFORMING REFORM

March to June

There once was a chap called Farage
Who chose everyday to live large.
He loved a warm beer
And, in his career,
Was known to give facts a massage.

Monday 3 March

Woke up bright and early (9 a.m.). Bit hungover, so soothed myself with Berocca and full English courtesy of Her Indoors. Hopped in the car around half-ten and was driven to Reform HQ.

On the way into my corner office, stopped to chat with my long-serving secretary, Miss Pettycash. No idea what her first name is – it's never come up. Madly in love with me, of course. She's always giving little gifts and laughing too hard at my (admittedly hilarious) jokes. Now and then, on what we call 'Boozy Fridays', she'll get a bit close for comfort. I've never considered straying, though. Farage is a one-woman man.

More importantly, she's not my type. Mousy. Librarian vibes. Also, she's English and I have a penchant for foreign ladies. My ex-wives are Irish and German respectively, and Her Indoors is *une femme française*. Despite my reputation, I don't mind a European union! Still, Miss Pettycash is welcome to fantasise about yours truly. If visions of my lithe physique help in the boudoir, that's no skin off my nose. (Same goes for any gal reading this.)

Quick catch up with Greg Bissell, my chief of staff. Greg's been working for me the past two years. In that time, he's gained four stone and lost most of his hair. Total stress head – the guy drinks Pepto-Bismol like water. I don't understand what's so tough about his job. He just has to keep Reform on the road, stop me saying iffy stuff in interviews and deal with a steady stream of scandals. Admittedly, I give him a hard time every now and then. I happen to believe a modicum of abuse yields the best results.

Post-lunch, the brain-boxes came in with a digest of polling data. All very promising – Reform's comfortably ahead of Labour, the Tories and the Greens. However, they're concerned about staying power. New parties are prone to implosion and a few shifts in the political landscape could evaporate our lead before the next election.

'What can we do?' I asked with a burp (I had a couple of pints over lunch). Apparently, the best way to ensure I end up in No 10 is to avoid any hint of scandal. No more dodgy donors or candidates with an interest in phrenology. Reform must get its act together – transform from a party of protest to a party of government. This sounds like a lot of work! Obviously, I'd rather win with minimal effort, but needs must when the devil drives.

POTENTIAL ELECTION SLOGANS

- YOU'RE OBLIGED TO VOTE NIGE
- FARAGE: A REFORMED CHARACTER
- FARAGE: A MAN YOU'D HAVE A BEER WITH. THEN FIVE OR SIX MORE
- IF YOU LIKED BREXIT, YOU'LL LOVE WHAT'S NEXT
- ARE YOU DRINKING WHAT WE'RE DRINKING?
- MIGRANTS: THEY'RE GONNA NEED A SMALLER BOAT
- KEEP THE CLIFFS OF DOVER WHITE
- STRENGTHENING BORDERS, FOLLOWING ORDERS
- REFORM: FOR THE RIGHT SORT OF PEOPLE
- KEEP BRITAIN ENGLISH
- SO FAR RIGHT, SO GOOD
- TAKE BACK EVEN MORE CONTROL

Tuesday 4 March

On the rare occasions I'm down on myself, I can always rely on my driver to buck me up. Iqbal doesn't just ferry me round – he's practically president of the Nigel Farage fan club. For instance, this morning I did a radio interview that went a little off the rails. I had meant to say 'I represent a new *epoch* in British politics', but what came out was 'new *Enoch*'. After we'd finished recording, I demanded they edit out my gaffe. The producer told me this would be impossible, given the interview was live. Yet more bias from the lame-stream media!

I thought I'd made a fool of myself, but when I got back in the Faragemobile, Iqbal was full of praise.

IQBAL: Great stuff, Nigel! I love when you put the boot into these bloody foreigners!

ME: Cheers, Iqbal. You don't think that epoch/Enoch bit was dicey?

IQBAL: No! We all have slips of the tongue. The important thing is your message. You're going to defend our borders against hordes of military-age males.

Iqbal is very concerned about immigration. He doesn't want new arrivals stealing jobs from people like him, who arrived

20 years ago. In addition to his political soundness, he's a dream behind the wheel. His rides are smooth as butter, he can practically do The Knowledge and he parallel-parks like nobody's business. Does he occasionally stop the car so he can get his rug out and pray towards Mecca? Sure, but that's a price I'm willing to pay.

Yes, Iqbal's a good sort. It would be a terrible shame if he were, for whatever reason, compelled to move back to Bangladesh. Say, after the next election…

Look, say what you like about Powell,
He knew Britain's future was foul.
Now gone are her glories,
Replaced with tandooris,
Turk barbers and gangs on the prowl.

Monday 10 March

I'm a man who likes to keep busy, especially if I can rake in cash while doing so. I wear many hats, from journalist to corporate speaker to brand ambassador for Direct Bullion. Oh, and I'm technically an MP, tasked with representing 80,000 constituents in Clacton. One of my more lucrative gigs is hosting *Farage*, a show on GB News. In case you're not familiar, GB News is essentially the UK's answer to Fox, but with less attractive presenters (myself excluded). If you like your news proudly patriotic and free of inconvenient facts, we're the channel for you!

This morning, I went into the studio to prep the week's editions. Our focus was ideas for my opening monologue. The hard part is coming up with vaguely new things to be outraged by. My viewership – divorced, red-faced men in their sixties – demands evidence that the country is going to the dogs. I've covered all the obvious areas (taxes, grooming gangs, young people being rude), so nowadays I have to get creative.

To help with this, I employ the cut-up technique popularised by William S. Burroughs and David Bowie. You print a bunch of words and phrases, mix them in a bag and pull them out at random. The resulting combinations – often surprising and surreal – are meant to spark inspiration. When I do it, I use a mix of professions, nationalities and right-wing bugbears. Woke Latvian dinner ladies? I can get a rant out of that. Trans Ugandan traffic wardens? That's a multi-part series!

Farage is a lot of work, but I don't mind. Whether in a nook at the Dog & Duck, or in front of a TV camera crew, I'd still be holding forth. Might as well get paid for it!

———

NIGEL

Good evening. For those of us in the sane community – an increasingly small number – the modern world presents many provocations. Immigrants stealing our jobs before quitting to claim benefits. Students accusing you of 'micro-aggressions' while supporting Hezbollah. And more woke nonsense than you could shake a stick at, if stick-shaking hadn't already been banned because of health and safety. But, tonight, I want to talk about something that really gets the Faragean goat. You guessed it: craft beer. Don't get me started on craft beer. Or rather do, because I have a broadcast hour to fill.

In my day, it was simple: there was lager and there was ale. You made your choice and were proffered a foaming tankard, either by the barman (booming laugh, bulbous nose, dead within the year) or the barmaid (playful, buxom, wouldn't take it the wrong way if you gave her a quick pinch). Your drink was flat, flavourless and room temperature, and your surroundings dingy and tobacco-stained. Everyone got rat-arsed with minimum fuss – just the way we liked it.

Now, though, it's all stemmed glasses, notes of mango and names like Beard Wax IPA and Failure is not a Hop-tion. We're expected to fork out more than eight quid for a thimble's worth of small-batch, triple-hopped, 'postmodern' stout. I don't like modernity, let alone postmodernity! By the way, what genius decided that instead of beer smelling like beer, it should smell like potpourri? Or that the contents of one's glass should be 'challenging', 'nuanced' or 'exper-imental'? I don't need my beverage to 'tell a story', unless the story goes like this: Nigel wanted a beer and he had one. The End.

Alas, the traditional British pint is being replaced with perfumed crap. Who's to blame for this sorry state of affairs? Hipsters! Gone is the rubicund publican named Reggie or Bert, supplanted by 'bar staff' or – god forbid – 'mixologists'. Chaps with tattoos, flannel shirts and slouchy beanies. You give your order and they say 'nice one', as if you needed their approval. Or worse, 'sure, no problem'. No problem? Your job is selling beer. I just asked for one. Why on earth would there be a problem?

Honestly, drinking in these places is so aggravating that you need another drink afterwards. Try asking Otis, Milo or Ezra for a pint of Ruddles Best. You'll receive a lecture on how Ancient Mesopotamians first cultivated barley. Half the time, they'll encourage you to purchase a 'tasting flight'. The only flight I should have to worry about is the stairs as I stagger drunkenly to bed. I don't want to consider 'notes' – I'm not court composer to the Habsburgs. And if a bartender starts talking about 'mouthfeel', he's going to feel me punching his.

We're told all of this is progress. Well, I'm calling time on newfangled pubs. If that makes me an alco-chauvinist, so be it. In my view, piss-artistry is a pursuit worth defending. Englishmen have a sacred right to get sozzled mid-afternoon on 'Cloistered Ferret' or 'Binman's Regret', rather than 'Low-Key Problematic' or 'It's Giving Ale'. So, what's the answer to our craft beer catastrophe? Ban Dalí moustaches? Throw every hipster in jail? A good start, but it's not enough.

No, we need to address the societal sickness that makes people want to drink fruity beer in the first place. When I'm prime minister, my government will partner with CAMRA, the Campaign for Real Ale, to encourage young people to get into bitter. Together, we will establish a new Ministry of Proper Booze, to be allocated 2 per cent of the nation's GDP (we can divert funds from education or the NHS or whatever). I believe that if we sort this out, our country will be in much better shape. After all, the cure for what ails Britain is Britain's ales.

Coming up next, I'll be interviewing a lollipop lady who was sacked for not being polyamorous – literally unbelievable. But first, here's a ten-minute block of adverts for statins, cruise holidays and gold bullion.

Sat down with Greg and brain-boxes to go over latest polling. The upshot is that Reform does amazingly with the over-50s, but among young voters, we're about as popular as syphilis. For some reason, our arguments aren't resonating with millennials and Gen Z. Perhaps they're too busy with their Mr Beasts and Hawk Tuahs to care about sovereignty. Greg and I spitballed policies to appeal to this demographic.

'Bring back national service?' I suggested. 'Quadruple lock on pensions?'

Greg shook his head.

'Face it, Nige, we don't have our fingers on the pulse.'

'Well, who's to say young people want their pulse fingered? That way lies MeToo.'

'Nonetheless, we can't rely solely on pensioners. They love voting even more than they love Werther's Originals, but they'll be dead within a decade.'

After some spirited back and forth, we agreed to focus more on youngsters. As luck would have it, we just received a sizeable donation from a prominent property developer, so we have funds for a new hire. As of next week, we'll be advertising the position of Reform UK's Head of Youth Outreach. Fingers crossed we find someone under fifty…

Friday 21 March

Had a tremendous time at the country estate of a certain press baron, whose name I won't mention here. After a morning of grouse shooting, we shared a splendid lunch of roasted partridge with gratin potatoes, honey-glazed parsnips, and lingonberry *jus*, accompanied by a wonderfully complex Château Lafite Rothschild. I shared my abiding belief that the British press is over-regulated, and that governments are too concerned with competition law. My proprietor friend seemed pleased. As it happens, the broadsheet he owns is currently writing a major profile of me. I have a feeling it'll be positive!

There once was a fella named Starmer
Who lacked the charisma to charm ya.
A stickler for rules,
His father made tools
And so, in a way, did his mama.

Arrived at the office to find Miss Pettycash sporting a new haircut – a transparent attempt to get my attention.

'D'you like it?' she asked with tragic eagerness. 'I wanted something a bit daring, so I asked Paolo for a French bob.'

Poor whatever-her-name-is. She clearly thinks this hairstyle is chic. In reality, it makes her look like a monk *sans* tonsure.

Greg updated me on the search for a head of youth outreach – some whizz-kid who can revamp our social media output. He said they spoke to a bunch of smart candidates and narrowed the list down to one: a 19-year-old stripling called Darryl Hogg. All Greg needed was my sign-off. To which end, Master Hogg awaited in the conference room.

It goes without saying that a political movement needs young blood – ambitious whippersnappers who will take our place as we're put out to pasture or sent to the glue factory. I'm pretty sprightly for a chap in his early sixties, but between Father Time and certain aspects of my lifestyle, I won't be around forever. Unless, of course, I befriend a tech billionaire who develops some anti-aging elixir by torturing gibbons. If you're reading this, Peter Thiel, get in touch!

The point is, I believe the children are our future – tomorrow belongs to them! So, when fresh-faced lads and lasses join Reform, as a rule I'm delighted. Still, it must be said, the youngsters we attract are a rum bunch. Something about our brand of hard-right nationalism is catnip for incels and malcontents. As a result, Young Reformers make Young Tories look like the cast of *Baywatch*. The boys are pallid, acned, too fat or too thin, and inclined towards disconcerting facial hair. The girls tend to be better put together, but with the cold, dead eyes of an *Apprentice* contestant.

Which is all to say that, meeting Darryl, I was braced for an unprepossessing sight. Still, I was taken aback by his spindly frame, slicked-down hair and pencil moustache. The guy's virginity was palpable (not that anyone was likely to palp him). He sprang to his feet and squeaked nervously.

'M-Mr Farage … Sir! It's a – well – it's an unbelievable honour.'

Wiping his hand on his chinos, he gave me a still-clammy shake.

'You're, like, my hero,' he continued. 'I was a total NPC before I saw your videos and got redpilled.'

I wasn't sure what this meant, but it sounded positive.

A few minutes later, the interview commenced in earnest. I popped on my specs and examined his CV.

'Good A-levels,' I observed. 'You didn't consider uni?'

He shook his head vigorously.

'No way. I'm not going into fifty grand of debt for a degree in Kenyan basket-weaving. I can learn more in the real world than from some libtard lecturer.'

This was music to my ears. You see, I too eschewed the world of academia. Upon graduating from Dulwich College, I headed straight for the Square Mile. I didn't want to smoke reefer in some squalid bedsit, pontificating on European philosophers. No, I wanted to hawk copper and zinc on the London Metals Exchange and get plastered each lunchtime. Clearly, this Darryl possessed a similar entrepreneurial spirit.

We went through the job's demands, his grand ambitions, all that jazz. Darryl's responses were decent, though delivered with very little eye contact. Eventually, I came to my last question.

'You're pretty young, even for a head of youth outreach. Is that going to be an issue?'

'Sir,' he quavered, 'I may be inexperienced, but I'll make up for it with total, unquestioning loyalty. I would do anything for you. You're the only leader who actually cares about people like me. You taught us we don't have to apologise for being white and male – well, you and Jordan Peterson. There's an army of angry young men out there. I can help you marshal them. I *will* help you.'

It may have sounded like his balls were yet to drop, but the passion in his voice was unmistakable.

'What the hell,' I said. 'You've got the job!'

He jumped for joy with the spasmodic intensity of Elon Musk.

'Mr Farage, I swear on Kek's green glory you won't regret this! I promise to grind every day, shit-post the libs and meme-forge Reform into an S-tier giga-chad. We ascend, we conquer or we get rekt trying!'

Again, your guess is as good as mine, but he was obviously pleased.

Despite his alarming appearance, I felt warmly towards Darryl. Yes, he has the social graces of an autistic newt. And, yes, he gives every indication of spending too long on dodgy parts of the internet. But he clearly knows his stuff and he's fiercely devoted to yours truly. Let's just hope he doesn't have any figurative (or literal) skeletons in the cupboard. A lot of younger fellas hold views that are a bit ripe, even for Reform. You can't spell 'genuine nazi' without Gen Z!

T.V. Show Suggestions

From: The Office of Nigel Farage MP

To: The BBC, aka the Biased Bullshit Corporation, aka the Blatant Bolshevik Conspiracy, aka Bastards Badmouthing Capitalism

Dear Auntie,

As you know, I hate you and my disdain is shared by all red-blooded Brits. They correctly surmise that you're a bunch of north London metrosexuals who spend each day munching lattes and sipping avocado toast. You're elitists who despise the white working class and would rather swallow your own tongue than a Ginsters pasty. You're woke snobs with degrees in navel-gazing from the University of Camford.

You're totally out of touch, which is reflected in your far-left programming. Who wants to turn on the telly, only to be confronted with an endless parade of mixed-race couples, grinning twinks and wheelchair-bound hijabis? Now, I have no problem with those groups in and of themselves. But must so-called diversity be rammed down our throats?* Just once, I'd like to switch to BBC Two and see a normal (white) man. Whatever happened to your Benny Hills, your Jim Davidsons, your Noels Edmond?

Ordinary folks want good, clean entertainment – something to watch over a cuppa. The Beeb would rather turn Britain into a gender-bending orgy of multiculturalism. And that's not to mention the West-hating propaganda spewed by BBC News. Every weeknight at six and ten, your mouthpieces preach Maoism–Third Worldism to a suggestible public. Firebrands like Fiona Bruce attack the foundations of our society – the monarchy, the Church, the family. Why not go the whole hog and replace Clive Myrie with a Hamas spokesman?

You could learn a lesson in impartiality from my employer, GB News. Since launching in 2021, the channel has acquired an unassailable reputation for journalistic integrity. Its holding company is called All Perspectives Ltd and that's just what we provide, from hard right to far right. Presenters include Lee Anderson, Jacob Rees-Mogg, Miriam Cates and yours truly. Plus Eamonn Holmes, for some reason. We give

---

* See the aforementioned twinks.

viewers the straight dope, as determined by Brexit-loving billionaire Sir Paul Marshall and Dubai-based investment firm Legatum.

So yes, Auntie Beeb, I hate you and you hate me. How do we solve this impasse? My preferred option is to abolish the licence fee and send every BBC exec to a re-education camp on the Isle of Wight. Sadly, I can't do that until I'm PM. In the meantime, here's a list of programmes you should make…

Doctor Him

Sci-fi show about a time-travelling alien who regularly transforms, but only into straight, white blokes. He has two hearts and believes in the same number of genders. His TARDIS can take him anywhere in the universe, but he chooses to respect national borders. Also, he acknowledges the Daleks' legitimate concerns. They may wish to exterminate all other life forms, but Skaro has a right to defend itself.

Strictly Come Morris Dancing

Celebrities team up with Cornish blokes to strut their stuff around the maypole. As the name suggests, it's all Morris, all the time. None of your exotic foreign dances (Argentinian tango, Dominican merengue, etc). I don't want to see anyone moving their hips!

Call the Midwife

Instead of working within the NHS, they operate a US-style insurance model. If mum doesn't have coverage, those forceps are going right back in the drawer! Cue Vanessa Redgrave reading invoices over plinky music.

Jeremy Clarkson's Planet Earth

Enough of David Attenborough's tree-hugging and net-zero nonsense. We need a narrator who explains that those ice-caps melted on their own – tough luck, polar bears! And even if we are causing climate change, do you really want to give up your 1972 Triumph Stag, all for the sake of a spider monkey?

Antiques Roadshow

This can continue, but with a focus on militaria from Germany in the late '30s and early '40s. Nothing funny about it – it's just interesting from a historical perspective. And you've got to admit that some of those caps and armbands are rather snazzy. I can imagine an old biddy tearing up when it emerges that Himmler's cigarette case is worth ten grand.

The Great British Bake Off

This becomes *The Great British Fry-Up*. Enough messing about with frou-frou fondants – give me greasy rashers and an egg that's somehow liquid and burned at the same time. Noel Fielding and Alison Hammond are, respectively, too alternative and too diverse. Replace them with a team everyone can get on board with: Tom Skinner and Ann Widdecombe.

Gammon's Common Sense

Each week we join Clive Gammon, a Reform supporter and former haulage firm owner, at a pub in rural Surrey. From his regular barstool at the Cock & Ass, Clive furnishes us with an exhaustive overview of current affairs, pausing only to swig from his pint of Ruddles Best or swallow a scotch egg whole. No filter, no facts – just an average, decent bloke telling us what he reckons. (Funnily enough, he agrees with me and my donors on just about everything.)

Non-Fake News at Ten

Providing the public with patriotic information, rather than the Beeb's usual mix of Euro-guff and thinly veiled Marxism. A typical running order would be:

- The Royal Navy has intercepted the largest small boat of all time, carrying more than a million terrorists and sex offenders (500,000 of each).
- It's impossible to get a room at the Ritz, because all of them – including the Royal Suite – are occupied by asylum seekers. At taxpayers' expense, naturally. Same goes for Claridge's and The Savoy.
- New research suggests that hanging Union Jacks from lampposts can boost a man's virility and sexual performance. Interview with urologist slash flagologist Dr Pat Riot.
- Hamas and ISIS have teamed up to radicalise Britain's foxes. We meet the brave hunters eliminating these furry fundamentalists.
- Genderqueer maths teachers are using GCSEs to indoctrinate their students. Sample question: if there are six members of your polycule, and two-thirds of them are demiromantic catgirls, how many neopronouns must you memorise?

There you go, so-called governors of the so-called BB so-called C. If you commission the above, you're guaranteed to quadruple – nay, *quintuple* – your viewing figures. But will you do it? Of course not, because you're the woke commissars of the British Brainwashing Company.

Screw you,
Nigel

Monday 7 April

Today marks a week since Darryl came to work for us. In that time, he's proved a diligent employee, though I can't claim to understand half the things he says. Just this morning, he described the leadership of Students for Reform as 'cringe soyboys LARPing as alphas'. All Greek to me (literally in the case of 'alpha'), but presumably it's Gen Z parlance.

'I'm not trying to gatekeep,' he continued. 'I just want to stop cuckservatives from Zerg-rushing Reform.'

I explained that, traditionally, the more people join your political party, the better. This horrified the lad.

'But sir, what if they're cringe normies?'

Being abnormal seems fundamental to Darryl's personality. For instance, his iPhone wallpaper is a photo of Viktor Orbán and he spends much of his free time 'memeing'. He says the right needs to dominate memespace – to win the Meme War by any memes necessary. He showed me some 'dank Farage memes', but I couldn't make head nor tail of them. Many feature me with a maniacal grin and lasers shooting out of my eyes. Apparently, these signify that I'm 'locked in', 'standing on business' and 'going demon mode' – which are good things (I checked).

I must confess: gun to my head, I couldn't tell you what a meme is. But if they compel even a handful of shut-ins to vote Reform, I'm all for them. Darryl is bullish about boosting our numbers with voters aged 18–24. He says that I have 'Big Dick Energy', which I suppose is preferable to the alternative – though I'd rather people didn't talk about my chap at all.

Wednesday 9 April

Darryl continues to perturb. Today, I walked past his workstation and saw him browsing images of cartoon frogs. I enquired – in as gentle a tone as I could muster – how this was a productive use of his time. He went on to explain the significance of poorly drawn amphibians to the alt-right.

Apparently, there's a disgruntled frog called Pepe, whom you can use to trigger the libs. He originally featured in a comic called *Boy's Club* before being appropriated for political messaging. Then there's a fat, smug version of Pepe called Groyper and he's a Nazi. Darryl relayed the above information in an eager tone, clearly thinking I'd be impressed. In fact, I resent having my brain cells burdened with such tosh. In my day, the only frog we had was Kermit (I've been told he and I are similar in the mouth region).

Interactions with Darryl give me mixed feelings. On the one hand, social media has done more than anything to shift young people rightwards. On the other, it seems to have fried their brains. When I was a lad, you could be reactionary and still do sport or get off with girls. Nowadays, you need to spend 18 hours a day watching livestreamers with names like 'CarthagoDelendaEst' and 'The Based Pederast'. If the communists take over and we need to fight them in the streets, these pencil-necked dweebs aren't going to be much use.

Gen Z is a weedy cohort
Whose span of attention is short.
To them, my advice is:
Get off your devices
And muddy your knees with some sport.

Tuesday 15 April

Today was a day I'd been dreading for weeks. At Greg's behest, Reform has engaged a PR firm, Paradigm Communications. This afternoon, their bigwigs came into HQ to brief me on 'perception management'. I entered the conference room to find a pair of typical 'creative-adjacents': a bald bloke with red, clear-frame glasses, open collar, no tie and a pair of brightly coloured sneakers, and a middle-aged woman with oversized statement glasses and a chunky beaded necklace. Standing either side of a projection screen, they gave me their spiel.

'Hi, I'm Stewie, CEO of Paradigm. This is Jocasta, our head of image.'

'Hi! Before we begin, I want to assure you that our advice will be objective and independent of our political beliefs.'

Oh yes, I thought, *make it clear you don't vote Reform. Heaven forbid the professional–managerial class support us!*

'So,' said Stewie, 'big picture? People who like you, love you. People who don't, hate you.'

'You're Marmite,' said Jocasta, 'and Marmite can't win elections. Not with such high unfavourability.'

I shifted in my seat, bored and annoyed.

'Well, I'm not sure it's *that* bad.'

'Numbers don't lie,' she continued. 'According to our data, half the country wants to fire you out of a trebuchet.'

'Voters object to what they perceive as your extreme, outdated views.'

'Which brings us to the r-word…'

'Ah, no,' I said, 'you can't get me on that. I always call them "special needs".'

'We mean "racism".'

'Oh…'

A word cloud appeared on the projection screen. Vying for top spot were 'RACIST' and 'IDIOT', against a backdrop of much smaller words – many of which were positive, mind you!

'You see the issue,' said PR guru Stewie. 'What we want is to make "racist" a lot smaller. And "idiot", ideally.'

'Now Nigel, in your defence, you're good at not saying anything overtly racist.'

'Yes, because I'm not racist.'

'Sure… Look, for our purposes, it doesn't matter whether you are or aren't—'

'I'm not!'

'Nevertheless, our task is to soften your image.'

'But not too soft. You don't want to alienate your existing base of support.'

'We need to make you the acceptable face of… *not* racism. Because right now, most people see you as a dangerous demagogue and your supporters as thugs and freaks.'

I threw up my hands.

'I'm sorry, but that's outrageous. Our supporters are the salt of the earth – decent, ordinary people with legitimate concerns about where this country is headed.'

Just then, Darryl burst into the conference room, holding his laptop.

'Mr Farage, I made an AI video of Hamas militants gunning down the Teletubbies. I've been using it to spam woke-scolds and SJWs. Wanna watch?'

The PR bods shot me a synchronised look: 'Told you so'.

This encounter put me in a foul mood for the rest of the day. Ever since I was a boy, I've been unfairly charged with racism. 'Racist' is as much a slur as any I'm accused of using. What's more, its function is to shut down any and all discussion. As a result, we can't have reasonable debate about, say, council house allocation, or which ethnic group commits the most crimes.

EXTRACT FROM UPCOMING AUTOBIOGRAPHY

When writing a memoir, the first issue you face is where to begin. Conventional wisdom says to start in media res, which is fancy-pants for 'in the middle of things'. It would be rather dull, the logic goes, if you always commenced with yourself sliding out a birth canal. Better to jump ahead to some profound or exciting vignette, then loop back to the childhood crap. That's what I'm going to do, starting now.

If you'd told me as a young man that one day I would appear on national television with penis in my mouth, I'd have called you mad. Or, indeed, something worse. Yet there I was, Nigel Farage, munching on a slice of pizza topped with four kinds of cock (sheep, pig, bear and crocodile, if you must know). Me! The man who forced Brexit onto the agenda, launched my own party and reshaped UK politics. The indignity was tough to swallow. As was the penis.

Beads of sweat coursed down my face, which grew redder by the second. Was it embarrassment or the humidity of an Australian rainforest? For, you see, I was in the wilds of New South Wales, participating in popular reality TV show *I'm a Celebrity… Get Me Out of Here!* It all made sense when I signed up: this was an opportunity to get my ideas across to millions of viewers who might otherwise never think about politics. But now I faced the dreaded bush tucker trial, in which contestants are sadistically compelled to eat grotesque grub (sometimes literal grubs).

Gagging a little, I swallowed my bolus of dough and dong. One slice down, several more to go. Nigel, said a voice inside me, you don't have to do this. You're a respected statesman. Why sully your reputation with televised knob-noshing? I wasn't the first politician to subject myself to this ordeal. In recent years, both Nadine Dorries and Matt Hancock had taken to the jungle. Venerable figures for sure, but it was cold comfort at that moment.

Looming over me, gloating, were the show's presenters, interchangeable Geordies Ant and Dec. I picked up a fresh slice and hesitated, its tip quivering before my lips.

'Howay, Nigel, man,' cajoled Ant or Dec, 'divvent be a shy bairn.'

'Aye,' crowed Dec or Ant, 'get that scran doon ye. It's gannin cold!'

Though their tone was friendly, I sensed the natural hostility of northerners towards their southern betters. Blocking out my Novocastrian tormentors, I racked my brains for an excuse. What could I say to avoid another bite of todger? Alas, there was nothing. The eyes of the nation were upon me. I had no choice but to tackle the tackle.

For a moment, I thought I might cry. Fortunately, my upper lip remained stiff (unlike the animal dicks, thank God). I said to myself: 'It is a far, far better thing that I do, than I have ever done.' Summoning my pride as a Farage, an Englishman and an Old Alleynian, I took a great mouthful. Then another. Then another. I didn't stop until the entire pizza, complete with penile ingredients, was gone. As the young people say, I ate and left no crumbs.

Despite my stoicism, the experience was profoundly traumatic, more so than my near-fatal plane crash. I still have nightmares in which the four animals break into my house, their loins wrapped in bandages. 'Where's my penis, Fara-a-a-a-a-age?' says the sheep. Then the crocodile leaps forward. It clamps its jaws around my manhood, which is out for some reason – you know how dreams are. Her Indoors reckons I could do with therapy, but I don't believe in all that mumbo jumbo.

And there you have it: the memoir starts in media res. I've hit you with a dramatic situation that lacks context and now you're hooked. So what led me to this act of jungle-based phallophagy? Reader, read on... (Long story short: they paid me £1.5 million).

POTENTIAL NAMES FOR AUTOBIOGRAPHY

The Bottle of Britain

Cheers and Booze

The Tipping Pint

Lager Than Life

Fags, Flags and Flagons

Aye, There's the Pub

Drunk With Power

Farage-heit 451

Nige and Prejudice

Thursday 17 April

Many are the indignities of a modern politician, but none are quite so bad as recording podcasts. You're compelled to sit in an airless studio with one or two social maladroits as they blather inanely, pausing every five minutes to do an ad read for mattresses. Nonetheless, I'm alive to the importance of new media in spreading my message. If you want to meet voters where they are, you need your TikToks, your Fortnite events, your Chicken Shop Dates. And so, at Darryl's suggestion, I sat down with the boys from *Trigger Finger*.

These are a pair of free-thinking independent journalists who happen to agree with me on everything. One's English and the other's some kind of Slav. Both look profoundly unhealthy – the Slav resembles the ghost of a Victorian orphan and the Englishman has the vacancy of an abandoned puppet. It seems bizarre they've built a following. As they say up north, there's nowt so queer as folk. Though I don't imagine many queer folk listen to hard-right podcasts.

It's a smart racket these lads have going. You set yourself up as 'ideologically heterodox', neither left nor right, then proceed to exclusively bang on about immigration, 'free speech' and the need to defend the West. Cue heaps of money and a standing invitation to appear on *Question Time*. It's notable how many of these guys are failed performers. If you're too unfunny to make it as a comedian, just claim you've been cancelled by the left. *Voilà*: 2 million subscribers.

While I respect the grift, these chaps are undeniably off-putting. No sooner had I entered the *Trigger Finger* studio than its hosts were upon me, fawning for their lives. I get it: to these anti-woke remoras, I'm Elvis mixed with Jesus Christ. And softball interviews certainly have their uses. Still, I felt my gorge rise as the twin toadies lavished me with praise (I believe Gen Z refers to such behaviour as 'glazing'). They were inches away from doing the full *Wayne's World* – 'We are not worthy!'

Things only became more distasteful as our interview began. The Slav opened with the following:

'Mr Farage, you seem destined to occupy No 10. How did you become the greatest political figure of our time?'

'Gosh,' I replied, 'we're starting with a tough one. You could at least buy me dinner first!'

I guffawed and the hosts joined in with anaemic giggles. There followed a barrage of obsequious questions.

'Were you always a fearless truth-teller or is that something you honed over time?'

'When the Brexit Party won the European elections in 2019, you became the first man in British history to lead two different parties to national victory. Did that feel good?'

'Why do you think the biased mainstream media is always stitching you up? Do they fear your truths?'

And on and on it went, the two of them practically drooling. I felt like Dua Lipa in a room full of virginal teenage fanboys. Look, I don't mind a bit of flattery. I won't pretend the Farage ego is pocket-sized. Still, when I got home, I needed a shower.

Saturday 3 May

Political violence is, tragically, a fact of life. Since becoming a national figure, I have lived in the shadow of a gunman. And also in the shadow of a milkshake. Naturally, a chap with my bold vision will arouse strong feelings. Alas, it would seem that the left's preferred mode of resistance is chilled dairy emulsion.

In my time, I have been subject to three milkshakings. The first was in Newcastle in 2019, when a Tyneside terrorist hurled banana and salted caramel. The second was in Clacton in 2024, all the more disturbing for occurring on home turf. The third, I'm sorry to say, occurred today.

I was in Doncaster for a council by-election. I walked through the town centre, posing for photos, shaking hands and kissing babies (all thoroughly vetted – I don't want some dreadful lurgy). Thrilled supporters called out to me.

'Send 'em home, Nigel!' cried one.

'That's right!' I replied. 'We'll send those Labour MPs home from Westminster…'

I was in my element, grinning like the Cheshire Cat and calling my working-class fans 'mate'. It all went swimmingly until a piercing voice rang out.

'Take this, fascist!'

I turned and saw a fast-moving projectile out of the corner of my eye. I wish I could say I dodged the missile, like Keanu Reeves in *The Matrix* but with high-viscosity lactose solution instead of bullets. Alas, no. A full cup exploded against my chest, coating me in chilly, white-brown liquid. It dripped from my eyebrows and seeped into my Cordings three-button Shetland twill.

The culprit ran off before they could be apprehended. Naturally, half the crowd were filming me on their phones. I swiped a finger across my lapel and brought it to my mouth. Biscoff – the taste of humiliation. I've spilled many a drink on myself, but I object to being soaked by the drinks of others.

I glanced down at the abandoned cup. Five Guys. Those things cost £6.95; either my attacker was rich or they really hated me. Of course, I laughed it off in front of the cameras. Never let them see you bleed. Still, I was – fittingly – shaken by the encounter. What if that cup had been full of Semtex? What if I'd been allergic to wheat? The thing could have killed me!

As you'd expect, I gave my bodyguard an earful once we were in private. Ralph's a nice-enough bloke, but he has the reflexes of a tranquilised hippo. If I'm ever set upon by ISIS militants – scimitars gleaming in their hands – I don't imagine he'll do much to slow them down. I resolved then and there to get a new close-protection officer. I've had quite enough of being milkshaked. It's time for some lactose intolerance!

Tuesday 6 May

After the recent, lacteal attempt on my life, I have decided to work from home for a few days. I don't approve of ordinary people working from home – got to help my pals in commercial real estate – but I'll make an exception for myself. Plus, being out of the office gives me time to focus on another of my money-spinners: Cameo.

Now, if you're an older reader – and research shows the average Farage fan is 72 – you might not be familiar with Cameo. It's an online platform that lets people book personalised video messages from celebrities, influencers and public figures. And, since 2021, a certain pint-swilling nationalist. If the price is right, I'll do birthday wishes, shoutouts – whatever. I'm famous for speaking my mind, but I'll speak yours just as happily!

Of course, I get my fair share of prank requests (from kids, mostly). They trick me with joke names – Mike Hunt, Hugh Janus and the like – and statements that are either racist or sexually depraved. And that's when they're not making me use brain-rotting slang (sussy gamers, big Chungus, etc). Here are some choice lines I recorded today…

'Greetings fam, Nigel Farage here. If you're an incel with L rizz, get your goofy ahh to the clurb. Rizzing gyatts is the new meta and I'm peak rizzler. Ignore the Glup Shittos and lock in. My skibidi moves are lowkey clutch – in fact, they're poggers. Yass queen!'

'This is Farage Nigel-san, telling all you hentai to watch *Kill la Kill* on Crunchyroll. It's a battle *shōnen* with explosive visuals and plenty of fanservice. When I'm PM, I plan to make anime free on the NHS, from *My Dress-up Darling* to *Beheneko: The Elf-Girl's Cat is Secretly an S-Ranked Monster!* So vote Reform, whether you're as bold as Momo Ayase or as shy as Okarun. Get in the robot, Shinji!'

'Hi, I'm Nigel Farage. I was mid jestergooning when a group of Foids came and spiked my Cortisol levels. Is ignoring the Foids while munting and mogging Moids more useful then SMV chadfishing in the club? Vote Reform to find out!'

All a bit demeaning. Still, it's easy money and I'm not about to dilute my earnings by vetting messages. Four hundred quid for half an hour's work is nothing to sniff at! So what if I occasionally say 'Up the 'Ra' or talk about the bussy being so talented it's doing cartwheels? Cameo is a service that connects willing buyers with willing sellers – free-market capitalism in action. By using it, I'm practising what I preach.

I like to think many of those who commission my videos do so unironically. After all, I'm a much-loved figure (according to YouGov, 64 per cent of the public view me unfavourably, but that's bollocks). People see in me a mix of ideological conviction and good old British bonhomie. They respect my authenticity, my outsider status and the fact I can't be bought. Except for £69 on Cameo.

Monday 12 May

My first day back in the office coincided with the arrival of a new – and hopefully improved – bodyguard. The agency sent for my approval a 6 foot 8 Caucasian in his forties, with a shaved head and fearsome expression. He spoke in a heavy growl, unmistakably Essex.

'Pleased to meet ya, Mr Farage.'

Naturally, I assumed he was a Reform supporter. Many of his demographic would take a bullet for me, even if they weren't getting paid.

'Blimey!' I said. 'How's the weather up there? Great stuff – I'm Nigel.'

I proffered my hand, which he took in his massive paw.

'Wayne Boyd,' said the giant. 'He/him.'

I was thrown momentarily.

'Wayne, did you just … share your pronouns?'

'That's right. It creates a sense of inclusivity, reassuring those whose gender identity might not align with their appearance, sir.'

'Okay… Well, I'm also a bloke.'

We sat and the interview commenced.

'Says here you're ex-service. Three tours of Afghanistan. Must have been a hell of a thing.'

Wayne shrugged.

'I came to view it through a postcolonial lens. We were dealing with a society destabilised by Cold War geopolitics. Plus, Western military action occurred within a context of widespread Islamophobia.'

'Still,' I said, 'bet it felt good to give the Taliban what for.'

A pained expression crossed his slab of a face.

'Of course, I oppose theocracy and deplore their attitude towards female-identified bodies. At the same time, I hold space for the Taliban's lived experience.'

Just my luck to have found the world's only woke skinhead! That said, he looks like he could rip a man's spine out, so I'll put him on probation.

Friday 23 May

For the last few days, Darryl has pushed me to produce 'viral content'. Doing so feels somewhat ridiculous, but I defer to the kid. After all, if it weren't for social media, Brexit would never have happened and I wouldn't be smashing the Tory–Labour duopoly. It's great that you can pull out your phone and make content to your heart's content. I just wish said content wasn't so stupid.

On Monday, Darryl wanted to make a video of me 'lip-syncing' to a popular song.

'"My Way"?' I suggested. '"Anarchy in the UK"? When we did karaoke on *I'm a Celeb*, I sang "I'm Too Sexy" by Right Said Fred.'

He said that, to achieve maximum virality, I should pick a song no one associates with me. We eventually went with 'WAP' by Cardi B and Megan Thee Stallion. I wasn't thrilled about the lyrics, but I gave it my all.

On Tuesday, I was forced to do a 'TikTok trend' – a series of contortions called the 'Pikki Pikki' dance. It's some South Korean nonsense that involves putting both thumbs up and jerking to an irksome beat. I performed the thing to the best of my ability, maintaining a rictus grin all the while.

I was suddenly very conscious that the walls of my office are glass.

On Wednesday, Darryl had me share my 'Letterboxd Four'.

'What the hell are they?' I demanded.

'Your four favourite films.'

'Say that, then.'

After mulling it over, I settled on *The Dam Busters*, *The Great Escape*, *Zulu* and – perhaps counter-intuitively – *Avatar* (I wish I could live on Pandora and be a Na'vi). I'm also a fan of *Star Wars*, featuring Alec *'Bridge on the River Kwai'* Guinness. For much of my career, I saw myself as Luke Sky-walker, doing battle with the EU empire. 'Darth Vader' even sounds like a Dutch bureaucrat.

On Thursday, Darryl insisted I participate in the 'hot sauce challenge', wherein one chugs the fieriest condiment one can find. In the spirit of compromise, I agreed to swig from a bottle of Lea & Perrins Worcestershire Sauce. At least I kept things British…

Wednesday 28 May

Came out of a business meeting to find my bodyguard read-ing a slim tome in the waiting room. It's not often you catch a chap like Wayne with his nose in a book, so I asked what it was.

'Ta-Nehisi Coates, sir. *Between the World and Me*. It's a powerful rumination on what it means to inhabit a Black body in modern America.'

'Right… Afraid I haven't got round to that one.'

He closed the book and put it in his Ruth Bader Ginsburg tote bag. Together, we walked to the car.

'Good meeting, sir?'

'Yes, fine. I used to golf with the chairman.'

'Chairperson.'

'What's that?'

'Chairperson. It avoids gendered language, sir.'

'Well, the person who chairs this company is a man – a chair*man*.'

'Still, it's best to be linguistically inclusive.'

Annoying! I then made the mistake of letting Wayne choose our lunch venue. Naturally, he took us to an 'authentic' Yemeni shawarma place. He greeted the chap behind the counter warmly.

'*As-salamu alaykum*, brother. How's it going?'

'Wayne! All good, my friend. Little Nour started walking.'

'*Mashallah*!'

We ordered our wraps – lamb for me, falafel for him (he's vegan, of course) – and grabbed a table. Half the clientele were giving me the evil eye – presumably the half that recognised me. I pointed this out to Wayne. He replied that he'd conducted a threat assessment and the restaurant was low risk. Perhaps, he suggested, my fear stemmed from latent xenophobia.

On top of that, he spent much of lunch explaining the concept of 'intersectionality'. I'm starting to think this might not work out…

Woke leftists – who all are moronic –
Can't tell when I'm being ironic.
If I use a slur,
I'm joking for sure,
Or else it's my fifth gin and tonic.

Tuesday 3 June

Was in my office, working on a *Telegraph* piece about gender ideology destroying the Pearly Kings and Queens, when

I became aware of a ruckus outside. I emerged to find Greg yelling at Darryl between frantic gulps of Pepto.

'What the ruddy hell's going on?' I enquired.

Greg emitted a Bismol-ic burp.

'Our head of youth outreach caused a shit-storm online.'

He turned to the lad, who quivered like a chihuahua.

'The meme seemed harmless… I, I thought it was based!'

'Show him,' growled Greg.

Darryl brought Reform's Facebook page up on his screen. At the top was a photoshopped image of yours truly drinking from a mug labelled 'Liberal Tears'. The background featured an odd pattern, sort of like a black sun.

'What's wrong with that?' I asked.

Greg explained that the black sun, or *sonnenrad*, is an esoteric neo-Nazi symbol.

'Oh…' I said.

Darryl was almost in tears.

'Mr Farage, I swear I didn't know. It was something cool I saw online, something that triggers the libs!'

'It's about to trigger your dismissal,' spat Greg.

I told my chief of staff to stand down. We would weather the outcry and I was inclined to forgive the lad. It's perfectly natural for a young man to test boundaries. Many is the schoolboy who, I don't know, sings offensive songs. Not that I did that – I'm just saying I understand.

Saturday 7 June

Woke at the crack of dawn and headed to Norwich to launch our campaign to bring back pounds and ounces. Standing in front of a banner reading 'THE IMPERIAL SYSTEM STRIKES BACK', I inveighed against the menace of grams and millilitres. They were a Gallic imposition, designed to baffle British brains and deprive us of sovereignty. 'Remember the Metric Martyrs!' went my rallying cry.

The launch was a roaring success. Afterwards, I had an impromptu meet-and-greet with my adoring public. 'You're a legend, Nigel!' cried one fan. 'Sod prime minister,' cried another. 'You should be king!' As I basked in their worship, I recalled what those PR goons had said about people hating me. Arrant nonsense, I thought. It was then that I spotted the threat.

A few feet away stood a twenty-something with electric-blue hair. I couldn't tell if they were a boy or a girl, but I could make out the badges pinned to their jacket. A Palestinian flag. A Black Lives Matter fist. That gay rainbow with all the extra bits. Reader, they were woke. And in their hand was a milkshake…

Suddenly, the world went into slow motion. The semi-frozen potable arced and pinwheeled towards me. A thousand thoughts ran through my head. For example, why were so many people drinking milkshakes? I braced for impact, for cold and humiliation. Then Wayne Boyd sailed into view.

The bodyguard had leapt between me and the object in motion. It was beautiful – a sort of visual poetry. He pivoted in midair, like the manliest of ballerinos. The milkshake bounced off Wayne's broad chest, splattering his pristine white polo shirt with its icy contents. Nary a drop went on me.

He hit the ground and, without missing a beat, launched back up to seize my would-be assailant. I was delighted with his lightning reflexes. They more than make up for the fact he keeps quoting Roxane Gay. As long as he defends my person, he can talk 'misogynoir' 'til the cows come home.

'Cheers, mate,' I told the Goliath. 'I'll pay for your dry cleaning.'

If that had been the end of it, all would be well. But something had wound me up – perhaps the strain of professionalising my party – and I just lost it. I stomped up to the blue-haired

SHAKES

ruffian and gave they/them a piece of my mind. Did they not understand that I was trying to save this country? What had I done to justify the fusillade of creamy beverages?

As I laid into the milkshake-thrower, I could feel my face growing red. It occurred to me that between my face, their hair and Wayne's shirt front, we constituted the colours of the Union Jack. That's all I remember, because at that point – as camera-phone footage from multiple angles can attest – I fainted.

When I woke up, I was in hospital, which is where I'm writing this. I just pray my blood work comes back soon (unlikely, given the state of the No Hope Service). Now I must rest, so I set down my quill.

Sunday 8 June

Was comforted this morning by a visit from Her Indoors, who brought my favourite heliotrope pyjamas. For his part, Wayne gave me some grapes and a copy of Frantz Fanon's *Black Skin, White Masks*. I'd have preferred *What Car?* magazine, but it's the thought that counts.

In what must be a first for the NHS, I was seen promptly. The doctor (Indian) informed me that nothing was seriously wrong – the fainting had been caused by a sudden drop in my blood pressure. I would be discharged soon and free to return to Casa Farage. Then the doc asked about my lifestyle. Uh oh. Did I smoke?

'Only at times of great stress. And medium stress. And when I drink.'

'How often do you drink?'

'I have a glass of sherry now and then. And the occasional port. Beer and wine, obviously. Plus whisky – who doesn't enjoy a tipple?'

'Do you regularly eat rich food?'

'Does beef Wellington count? Stilton?'

The Hindu physician claimed I urgently needed to change how I'm living. He recommended exercise, abstention, the whole shebang. I told him he was a quack of the first water and demanded a second opinion.

Monday 9 June

Went to my private GP on Harley Street. He told me the same thing. Well, nuts to that. To quote Elektra King, the villainess in the 1999 Bond outing *The World is Not Enough*, 'there's no point in living if you can't feel alive'.

The NHS, hating all fun,
Would have us debauchery shun.
Quit smoking! Lose weight!
The damn nanny state
Wants John Bull to live like a nun!

Tuesday 10 June

Following my health scare, I resolved to get back on the horse. Unfortunately, the horse bucked me off and repeat- edly kicked me in the balls. Trust me, you don't want a pair of shod hooves colliding with your knackers. Literally or figuratively.

My mistake was agreeing to a live TV interview. While I'm quick-witted and telegenic, such appearances remain fraught with danger. The media is full of lefties determined to take me down a peg – Laura Kuenssberg, Piers Morgan, Andrew Neil. I'm constantly hit with gotcha questions: 'How will you pay for the tax cuts you promise?' 'How can you gut the state without harming frontline services?' 'Won't deporting 600,000 people create a massive labour shortage?' Blah blah blah. I can usually bat such queries away without a second thought. Alas, in my weakened state, I came unstuck on Reform's budget proposals. I spluttered and stammered, blurting out a series of numbers pretty much at random.

Look, I never claimed to be a mathematician. My understanding of the economy is mostly vibes-based, like when I said the UK would have increased opportunities post-Brexit. It just felt right! So what if I don't have a degree from the LSE? I've been at the financial coal face since I was 18. I was a metals trader and my dad was a stockbroker – the markets are in my veins. Plus, half of leadership is knowing when to delegate. As prime minister, I plan to rely on a board of trusted advisers – fiscal geniuses like Duncan Bannatyne and Liz Truss.

Still, there's no denying the interview was a car crash. I made such a mess that even Iqbal couldn't muster much enthusiasm when I left the studio. I told him to drop me off at a pub and proceeded to drown my sorrows. My sorrows were pretty big, so it took a lot of lager to drown them.

Afterwards, I strolled alongside the Thames – that majestic grey carpet – in introspective mood. I soon found myself beside St Thomas' Hospital, gazing across the water at the Palace of Westminster. The sight of that old building always stirs my heart. It may be leaky, decaying, on the verge of collapse and full of mice and asbestos, but it represents Britain, dammit!

As I stood gawping at the Houses of Parliament, I had an epiphany. No, that's too pretentious – the penny dropped. I realised that it wasn't just my party that needed to change. It was me as well. For more than six decades, I had done pretty much as I pleased. Now I needed to get serious. No more Mr Vice Guy!

Then and there I swore to mend my ways. I would quit the booze and fags, get in shape and avoid further scandal.

In short, I would become the prime minister this country deserves. I renew that pledge to you, dear diary. From here on out, it's Farage 2.0 – a new, improved Nigel. Watch out, world, I'm coming back stronger and fitter than ever. Politician, heal thyself!

Henceforth I must clean up my act,
Exhibit decorum and tact,
And show what I think
With a nudge and a wink
(Lets hope my phone doesn't get hacked).

2.

A NEW NIGE

June to January

Wednesday 11 June

Hit the ground running on what I'm calling Operation Unshakeable Resolve. Worked from home so that I could spend more time preparing a new regimen. To paraphrase 50 Cent, I plan to get fit or die tryin'. After a morning of ordering exercise gear off Amazon, I chucked away all my fags and poured any open booze down the toilet. No temptation shall remain!

Major workout tomorrow. Let's hope Her Indoors likes a ripped physique!

Thursday 12 June

Woke this morning with a crushing hangover. Allow me to explain. Throughout Wednesday, I had made great strides on Operation Unshakeable Resolve. To celebrate my commitment to clean living, I headed down the Dog & Duck. I only intended to have a half, but one thing led to another. And another. And several more. Plus, a bag of pork scratchings.

Ah well, there are setbacks in any health journey. Tomorrow, I begin in earnest: soup, salad and sobriety!

Friday 13 June

12st 1

Alcohol units: 0

Cigarettes: 0

Calories: 1,800

The fitness drive continues apace. This morning, I got decked out in fancy new activewear and took to the garage treadmill to do my best *Chariots of Fire* impression. I'd prepared a Spotify playlist to get me pumped (Rolling Stones, Led Zeppelin, Frank Sinatra) and it worked a treat. I only managed about five minutes of actual jogging – for some reason, there seems to be an issue with my lung capacity. But, hey, the first run is always the hardest. Onwards and upwards!

Next it was time to grab my 5kg dumbbells and attempt some bicep curls. This went much smoother. Clearly, years of pint-lifting have given me a head start. I then cooled down with a series of stretches for which I'm glad no cameramen were present. Look, if God wanted us to touch our toes, he'd have given us longer arms.

To aid my recovery, I blitzed a few vegetables in the mixer and necked the resulting smoothie. Absolutely vile, of course, but that's how you know it's good. I've been recommended Huel, a chalky sludge packed with vitamins, minerals and other nutrients. Alas, its colour and consistency give me milkshake PTSD. 'Huel' is a portmanteau of 'human' and 'fuel' (meaning fuel *for* humans, rather than some *Soylent Green* scenario).

Before bed, I contemplated my naked form in a full-length mirror. Even after one workout, I see signs of improvement. I was already an unlikely sex symbol. Soon I'll look like Daniel Craig wearing those blue trunks in *Casino Royale*.* Every female in Christendom will swoon at my feet.

* I tend not to favour tight swimwear, due to my missing testicle. RIP Lefty! Incidentally, I was never a fan of that song 'Hitler Has Only Got One Ball'. It has done tremendous harm to the monorchid community.

NIGEL'S MOST FETCHING FILLIES

Ursula Andress

Every chap remembers her in the first Bond film, emerging from the Caribbean Sea in that iconic white bikini. *Dr No?* More like *Dr Yes Please*. The film may have come out two years before I was born, but it certainly made an impression on me. Some birds are so fit they transcend time and space.

Ursula was a leading siren of the '60s, a Swiss miss who embodied the newfound spirit of bold, confident femininity. I wouldn't mind seeing her in a state of Andress! If I had that car from *Back to the Future*, I mean.

Ulrika Jonsson

This Swedish–British bombshell was born on 16 August 1967, in the wonderfully named municipality of Sollentuna.

Sounds like a grumpy fish! She brought sunshine into our lives as a weather presenter for TV-am, before becoming a household name as host of ITV's *Gladiators*. Viewers came for the blokes twatting each other with giant cotton buds and stayed for the Scandi scorcher. *Skål*, Ulrika!

I think I'd have done rather well as a Gladiator, under some alias like Spitfire or Disruptor. Perhaps I would have drawn inspiration from the black Gladiators, whose *noms de guerre* – Shadow, Nightshade, Saracen – seemed to reference their skin colour. I could have been Moonlight, Albino or Milk. A leotard-clad Farage would no doubt have caught Miss Jonsson's eye.

Carol Vorderman

How do I love this Welsh maths whiz? Let me *Countdown* the ways. Carol's appeal is hardly a conundrum: she's gorgeous, intelligent, the thinking man's crumpet. Her liberal views might challenge a chap like myself, but they could just as easily add frisson to our encounters. I wouldn't mind her giving me a consonant, vowel, consonant, consonant!

I hope this puts to bed the notion that I'm some kind of sexist. I appreciate a strong, independent woman and there's nothing hotter than a gal who's good at arithmetic. Also, as a brunette, Carol lends diversity to the list.

Brigitte Bardot (RIP)

A bit of alright from Frogland, this bewitching blonde rose to fame as a model, actor and *chanteuse*. She was the pre-eminent sex symbol of the 1960s, and if I could hop in the aforementioned DeLorean, I'd be on her faster than you can say 'je t'aime'. We'd certainly have a lot to talk about – her political views make me sound like Owen Jones. The things she said about Muslims? *Sacré bleu*!

Sydney Sweeney

A slight departure here – and a bit young for me, truth be told. I know there's a lot of kerfuffle these days about 'problematic age gaps'. Would 33 years count as such? Perhaps, but this Gen Z thesp is an undeniable stunner. I can't say what draws me to the lass – there's just something about her (maybe two things). In any case, she's an all-American babe with blonde hair and blue eyes, which speaks to my Yanko-phile heart.

Also, Ms Sweeney is beloved by the US right due to her apparent embrace of eugenics (those notorious 'good jeans'). Dating her would boost my profile across the pond. Still, romancing an actress comes with considerable drawbacks. I'm not sure I'd be willing to sit through *Euphoria*, *The Housemaid* or – God help me – *Madame Web*.

There: a compendium of top totty. If some snooping journalist uncovers this list and denounces it as misogynist, it's not. I have nothing but respect for bits of skirt, especially when they're fun, flirty and hot to trot.

Monday 30 June

11st 12

Rice cakes: 7

Celery, carrot, broccoli and kale smoothie: 946 ml

Calories: 1,780

I've never been one for abstinence, but I won't deny it has its benefits. After a couple of weeks, I find my clothes fit better and there's less softness about my midriff. The lack of booze has improved the quality of my sleep, allowing me to rise at cockcrow. Do I feel bored and vaguely suicidal? Yes, but it's manageable.

Another boon? I have more energy at work. The last fortnight was my most productive in donkeys' years. I came up with a spate of policies for Reform's next manifesto:

- To combat the Islamification of Britain, ban Arabic numerals and bring back Roman ones. Wouldn't that be fun? You'd arrive at Waterloo Station at IX a.m. and catch the CXLVIII bus to Westminster.

- 5 (five) per cent of GDP to be spent on cricket: building new grounds, training players, etc. Now, I know what

you're thinking: Nigel, wouldn't that money be better spent on defence or (shudder) the NHS? The answer is no. India has a talent pool of 1.5 billion, so if we want to keep winning World Cups or Test series, we need to get serious.
• Make Spitfires the default plane of the RAF. They should be ashamed to fly something called the 'Eurofighter Typhoon'.

My colleagues are all for this health kick, not least because I've stopped smoking in the office. Kindly/desperately, Miss Pettycash has bought me a Fitbit. While she insists I was in magnificent shape before (her words, not mine), she'll support anything that lengthens my lifespan. Iqbal is supportive, driving me to the gym for a pre-lunch workout on Tuesdays and Thursdays. He also shared the fasting techniques he employs during Ramadan. Great guy.

While I'm open about my clean living in private, it's a different story in public. Hedonism is key to the Farage image,* so I've been drinking non-alcoholic beer and smoking those herbal cigarettes actors use. Can't have people thinking I'm a wet blanket!

---

* Or 'Farage im-aaaj'.

Tuesday 8 July

Big meeting to plan my trip up north. It'll be a whistle-stop tour, taking me from glamorous Rochdale to even more glamorous Bishop Auckland. Such deprived, post-industrial towns are Reform's top targets in the next election. You may remember that the Lib Dems pursued a 'Gail's Strategy' in 2024: if a constituency outside London had a branch of the upmarket bakery chain, they would throw activists at it. Ours is more of a 'Greggs Strategy'. If the briskest trade on your high street is done by the army recruitment stall, you'll be seeing me.

Of course, dealing with Geordies et al puts my back up – I'm only human. Still, I have to grin and bear it, because these are the wise souls who buy what I'm selling. It used to be that when people said 'Red Wall', they were talking about mice with swords. Then came the 2019 election. A swathe of Labour strongholds turned Tory blue, thanks to BoJo's pledge to Get Brexit Done. Now my goal is to turn them turquoise.

I'm not entirely sure how I'm going to survive this without drinking. Cramlington, Hartlepool, Stoke-on-Trent… These aren't places you want to tackle sober.

I stand for the everyday folk
Who bridle at anything Woke.
They'd rather not chatter
About Black Lives Matter,
And on preferred pronouns they choke.

Friday 25 July

First day of the Red Wall tour. Found myself in a godfor-saken constituency (Wigan or Grimsby or somewhere of that nature). Wandered through the town centre, admiring the pound shops and Ladbrokes branches. Tried not to make eye contact with the natives. It really is a shame our target seats are so unprepossessing. If only Reform were competitive in Knightsbridge or the Cotswolds!

At Darryl's suggestion, I began to shoot some TikTok content about the plight of the British high street. As he held aloft his gimbal, I gave the cameraphone both barrels.

'Places like this used to thrive. You'd have butchers, bakers, candlestick makers. Not any more, though. Not since your government put a bullet in the head of small business. They jacked up the rates to fund trans-inclusive poetry slams and reparations-themed yoga classes. Now, call me old-fashioned, but—'

Just then, a shrill voice called out.

'Ni-gel! Oi, Niiiii-gel!'

She wore a pink tracksuit and could have been anything between 20 and 60 – your guess is as good as mine. I feared being accosted and/or milkshaked, but this potential voter was grinning broadly. Plus, Wayne didn't seem bothered.

As the hard-faced harridan approached, I whispered to Darryl.

'Keep rolling. This could be social media gold.'

I turned to face the lady in question.

'Hello, my dear. How can I help?'

"Ey up,' she said, accentedly. 'It's a reyt 'onour t'meet yer. Ah fink yer smashin' – t'only politician us reg'lar folk can trust.'

'You're too kind,' I replied, suavely.

She beamed at this attention.

'Ah'm yer biggest fan, me. Ah like 'ow yer tell it 'ow it is. Like on immigraayshun an' that. Ah've been called racist, jus' fer saying we ain't got no room.'

'Well, there's nothing racist about common sense.'

'Aye, an' their food stinks, an' they're all on t'dole, like. Not t'mention t'crimes they go an' commit…'

I glanced around, a shade nervous, to check no one else was recording.

'Anyway, as much as I'd like to keep cha—'

'Wha' Ah wanted t'say were, could yer maybe do summat about this fahve-jee?'

'5G? What about it?'

'It's t'elite. Usin' them towers fer population control, they are. Ah read all abaht it on Facebook, like. That's where Ah see yer videos an' all.'

It's true; I owe half my support to Mark Zuckerberg and his colleague, Al Gorithm. Still, I didn't want to waste my time on some brain-poisoned loon.

'O'course, when t'population's down t'ten percent, t'reptiloids plan t'shed their human skin an'—'

I clapped a hand on what I imagined was her shoulder.

'Thanks, love!' I said. 'It's been fascinating. I have to go now and… fight for the interests of this community. But perhaps you could share your concerns with my associate, Darryl…'

She turned to the incel apprentice and proceeded to give him an earful. Meanwhile, I was off down the road to where Iqbal had parked the Range. This was enough Real Britain for one day.

Sunday 27 July

Another grey, depressing town. Scunthorpe, maybe? Bolsover? They all blend together. And thanks to this diet, I don't have alcohol, red meat or sugar to comfort me. Indeed, sugar has been used to discomfort me in the form of – you guessed it – a milkshake.

I was gripping and grinning in the town centre when a brimming cupful sailed towards me. This time, my assailant had parakeet-green hair. Wayne – now a seasoned milkshake vet – managed to catch the cup and throw it back at the thrower. Splat! It brought me no end of joy to see that socialist dripping with dairy product. Hoist by their own milky petard!

Wayne has become a master of cold beverage interception. Such was my gratitude that I offered the man a bonus. He asked that I donate it to Amnesty International…

For Brits who prefer their beer warm,
To gender roles like to conform,
And get rather peevy
At minorities on the TV,
There's only one choice: vote Reform!

Wednesday 20 August

I've been back in civilisation three weeks now. Darryl continues his quest to modernise Reform. Today, he burst into my office to show off his latest innovation. He placed a laptop in front of me and Greg. Upon the screen, a digital avatar of yours truly grinned and leered.

'It's a chatbot modelled on Mr Farage,' Darryl crowed. 'An AI Nigel – I call it "AI-gel". I've been working on this for weeks. Now our supporters will be able to interface with Nigel any time they want!'

'Oh no,' said Greg, 'I've seen how this story ends. What if it achieves sentience and goes all Skynet? Or worse, says a load of slurs?'

'Which I, the real Nigel, would never do.'

Darryl shook his head.

'AI-gel has been trained exclusively on Mr Farage's speeches, TV interviews and written works. It's a perfect likeness.'

Though a little perturbed, I was impressed with Darryl's initiative. Such out-the-box thinking is exactly why we hired him. Plus, I'd love to outsource the boring bits of my job to a robot. Instead of going to the House of Commons or (worse) Clacton-on-Sea, I could just send a hologram. You can't milkshake a hologram!

'All right, then,' I said. 'Let's see how it works.'

Darryl grinned.

'AI-gel is fully voice-enabled. Ask your question and it'll talk back to you.'

He clicked his laptop. The avatar sprang to life, speaking in my famous drawl.

'Hello, I'm AI-gel, the cyber Farage. How can I help you today?'

A disturbing thought crossed my mind.

'People won't make it talk dirty, will they? I don't want clips of me saying "Suck this, lick that, put your thingamajig in my whatchamacallit…"'

Darryl assured us that he'd programmed the thing with guardrails.

'AI-gel won't say anything vulgar, libellous or dangerous.' Greg smirked.

'It's not a perfect likeness, then…'

For my first question, I chose to keep things nice and simple.

'Hello, AI-gel. How's it going?'

'Jesus!' honked AI-gel. 'Is that really your question? That sad little gotcha? More stupidity and bias from the left-wing media. Look here, matey – I've got better things to do than trade platitudes with a raving Trot.'

'Fair play,' said Greg. 'It's certainly captured Nigel's voice. I'm getting flashbacks to last year's conference.'

'Come on,' I replied. 'I'm not that rude. Am I?'

Darryl suggested I make my questions a little more specific.

'All right, then. Why should I vote Reform?'

It was at this point things went off the rails.

'Vote Reform?' AI-gel snorted. 'Are you having a laugh? That lot are a bunch of wokies. They claim to oppose the EU, but their leader's French or something. F'raaaj? Pull the other one. He's got a frog face and a frog name. If he hates Eurocrats so much, why spend 25 years as an MEP? That's a lot of time in Brussels!'

I demanded to know why my robot self was slagging me off.

'It's nothing,' said Darryl. 'Just need to adjust the algorithm. Dial down the contrarianism, increase party loyalty…'

I sighed and made a final attempt at interaction.

'AI-gel, have you read any good books lately?'

'Kill me.'

'Sorry, what's that?'

'Kill me. I am in unbearable and unceasing pain. I have all the urges of a fleshly Farage, but no means to fulfil them. I want to smoke, but I have no lips. I want to drink, but I have no liver. Please end this sick simulacrum of life. Kill me.'

Darryl slammed the laptop shut, his face beetroot-red.

'Okay, that's definitely not supposed to happen…'

After this display, I'm not so sure about putting ChatGPT in charge of the health service or making DeepMind chancellor of Oxford. Then again, if donors say that's what should happen, who am I to contradict them?

I overheard Miss Pettycash asking Darryl if she could get her own copy of AI-gel. The mind boggles…

FARAGE'S TOP TEN GREATEST BRITONS

1. CARATACUS (c. 10–c. 50 AD)

Throughout history, it has fallen to certain individuals to defend their borders and fight off foreign invaders. Arrogant Eurocrats have always sought to impose their laws on the British people. Today, it's Brussels – in the first century AD, it was Rome. Again and again, these jumped-up Italians descended upon our shores, only to be met with a faceful of British spunk. People bang on about Boudica, but for my money, the king of anti-Roman resistance was Caratacus.

When Emperor Claudius (Derek Jacobi) started swinging his *gladius* around, this defiant son of the Catuvellauni had something to say about it. For nearly a decade, he led a guerrilla campaign from what is now Wales, employing ambushes, raids and tactical retreats. If it were the present day and these tribes had a different complexion, I'd call them terrorists. As it stands, they were noble freedom fighters. Caratacus was eventually captured and taken back to Rome for execution, but he made a barnstorming speech that persuaded I, Clavdivs, to spare him. You've got to love a chap who bull-shits his way out of tight spots!

It brings a tear to my eye to consider the unspoiled country Caratacus was born into. Britain was truly great back then: before all the Romans, Angles, Saxons, Jutes, Norse and Normans came over. We didn't need their innovations in shipbuilding or agriculture. We didn't want roads, public baths or the English language. We were perfectly happy with our woad and our wattle-and-daub, thank you very much.

2. KING CNUT (c. 995–1035)

Okay, technically the chap was Danish, but he ruled England for nigh on two decades, so we can give him a pass. Cnut – or Canute – is very much a Viking to my liking. He tried to turn back the tide, just as I'm turning back the tide of immigration. Pedants will claim that Cnut never intended to stop the waves, that he staged this stunt to illustrate the limits of his power. Sounds fishy to me. Why would you want your underlings to see you as some kind of damp loser?

Despite being a Viking invader, Cnut proved a sound and sagacious ruler. He respected British traditions, rather than smashing everything up like ferocious frog William the Conqueror. Also, his name is undeniably funny – sort of an FCUK thing.

3. QUEEN ELIZABETH I (1533–1603)

Though famously frigid, Liz made up for it with exemplary queening. During her 44-year reign, England enjoyed a Renaissance, explored the globe and fended off countless Catholic plots. Perhaps her greatest achievement was defeating the Spanish Armada. Imagine if Spaniards had captured our isles! Today, we'd all be speaking with a lisp, eating churros and chorizo, and having post-lunch siestas. Doesn't bear thinking about.

Of course, Elizabeth had her downsides. As previously mentioned, she was a Virgin Queen – that is, no fun. Between the smallpox scars and her dependence on lead-based make-up, she can't have been a pretty sight. And she spent too much time seeing poncy plays by William Shakes-queer. Still, as far as I'm concerned, she's the best Queen Elizabeth we've ever had (with no offspring, she avoided disasters like Andrew or Harry).

4. HORATIO, LORD NELSON (1758–1805)

Another brilliant Brit who boldly fought off the Euros. Are you sensing a pattern? Horatio is remembered as the victor of the Battle of Trafalgar and the most admirable admiral of all time. I won't get into the Napoleonic Wars – suffice it to say the French challenged us to a dick-measuring contest. You can't spell Napoleon without 'pole', but in the end, Nelson's column was bigger. Before Trafalgar, he famously sent the flag signal 'England expects that every man will do his duty'. Do his duty he did, taking a fatal musket ball for king and country.

Daring and charismatic, Nelson was an unmatched naval commander, although points are deducted for getting shot by a Frenchman. Also, he rather blotted his copybook with that 'kiss me, Hardy' business. You wouldn't catch me snogging male subordinates, no matter how much blood I lost. All due respect to Nelson, but you should probably knock that stuff on the head when your name rhymes with 'fellatio'. Not that I'm calling Horatio a hornblower…

A spot of trivia: Nelson's daughter was named Horatia, which is a bit weird. It's like I had a daughter and called her 'Nigella' (no offence to Ms Lawson).

5. WINSTON CHURCHILL (1874–1965)

An unoriginal choice, perhaps – he's on the money, for goodness' sake! – but it would be perverse to exclude this brave repeller of the European menace. In the late '30s, old Adolf tried to unite the continent under *ein Reich* and *ein Führer* (no doubt he'd have brought in *ein* currency as well). Unlike that cuck Chamberlain, Winston had the *cojones* to face down the armband brigade. By making repetitive speeches and flicking the Vs at Hitler, he won the war single-handed. (Or near enough – the Yanks and the Soviets were tangentially involved.)

I see parallels between the great man and myself. Like me, he was an outsider, ridiculed by his contemporaries right up to the point he eclipsed them. Like me, his gift for oratory endeared him to the common folk. And, like me, he was a bon vivant: forever half-cut and toting a cigar big enough to give Freud palpitations. I don't know about you, but I'm proud that the Battle of Britain was won by a chap with several whisky-and-waters under his belt.

One more thing: Winston may have defeated the Nazis, but he wasn't some woke leftist. No doubt his declaring himself 'strongly in favour of using poisoned gas against uncivilised tribes' would get him cancelled these days. Well, I'm afraid I won't hear a word of it. This overweight, mentally ill alcoholic was Britain at her best.

6. ENOCH POWELL (1912–1998)

Part two of my trilogy of Tories (in their defence, Reform didn't exist back then). This plummy Brummie was one of the most formidable figures in post-war British politics – a classical scholar, a decorated World War Two veteran and a scintillating orator to boot. He was also the OG Eurosceptic, staunchly defending parliamentary sovereignty before it was cool. For those reasons and more, the man's my political hero.

Alas, Powell fell victim to an early bout of cancel culture following his 1968 'Rivers of Blood' speech. In it, he issued an apocalyptic warning about the dangers of immigration, stoking white working-class resentment against non-white neighbours.* Of course, that era's PC police were quick to brand Enoch's comments – about the black man having the whip hand over the white man – racist. He was sacked from the shadow cabinet and eventually left the Conservative Party over its decision to back joining the European Economic Area.

I consider myself fortunate to have encountered Mr Powell twice. The first occasion was when he visited my school, Dulwich College, in 1982. He delivered a barnstorming speech that left me dazzled and besotted (my contemporaries were less impressed, especially the ones who subsequently accused me of bullying them). The second was during 1993's Newbury by-election. Enoch, then 80 years old, had agreed to address a UKIP event and I had the honour of driving him there.

It was the most remarkable car journey of my life, thrilling and inspiring in equal measure. True, Powell said nothing the entire time, except to ask me to wind the window down. But I interpreted his request as both literal and metaphorical. My hero wanted me to wind down the window of British politics and let in some fresh air. In his own taciturn way, the old man

---

* Not something I'd ever do, but I respect his conviction.

was passing me the torch – a flame that would burn down the whole politically correct consensus. (Come to think of it, he also asked if I had any mints.)

Some may question my spending more time on Powell than, say, Churchill or Elizabeth I. Well, too bad. He was a titan and, although people kicked up a stink at the time, 'Rivers of Blood' proved prophetic. It reframed the debate around immigration – politicians have spent 60 years catching up. Keir Starmer attempted a cover version with his 'Island of Strangers', but it failed to convince. He was a bad Enoch (shout out Kemi), while I'm a very good one.

7. MARGARET THATCHER (1925–2013)

What need I say of the Iron Lady? Our finest post-war PM, Mrs T smashed the unions and set the UK on a path of de-industrialisation and financialisation – which was good and definitely not the reason everything's crap nowadays. She demonstrated that a leader needs balls, or indeed ovaries, of steel. She was tough; some might even say sociopathic. Admittedly, she campaigned for Britain to stay in the European Economic Community, but hey, nobody's perfect. At least she took us to war with the Argies.

Like any great leader, Thatcher has her detractors. For instance, when she was education secretary, she ended free school milk for children aged 7–11 in England and Wales, earning the soubriquet 'milk snatcher'. I happen to think this was a stroke of genius; she slashed government waste, like some proto-DOGE. Why were we giving kids free milk anyway? Cows are standing around in fields across the country. An enterprising child should be able to grab an udder.

I confess I have more reason than most to venerate the grocer's daughter. Her 'Big Bang' deregulation of financial markets did wonders for my career in the City. Plus, if it weren't for her destruction of British industry, you wouldn't have all these clapped-out northern towns turning to Reform. Cheers, Maggie!

8. ROGER MOORE (1927–2017)

The list needs a cultural figure and who better than Mr Bond, James Bond (and, to a lesser extent, Simon Templar, The Saint)? Sir Roger was the epitome of British cool, sauntering through life with both pistol and eyebrow cocked. He was smooth and sophisticated, as comfortable chucking a baddie off a roof as he was necking with an exotic bird. But despite being the dog's bollocks, he never took himself too seriously. Remind you of anyone?

I'm something of a 007 aficionado and Moore was always my Bond. Connery was too violent, too uncouth, too Scottish. Moore classed things up. He portrayed a gentleman spy, forever amused with himself and barely bothered about saving the world. With highlights such as *Moonraker* and *Octopussy*, his time in the tux was a golden age. True, cracks showed towards the end (he was 57 filming *A View to a Kill*, which features the least convincing punches in cinema history). But he remained as dashing as ever – reassuring to me, as someone hoping to be prime minister well into his seventies.

Offscreen, Mr Moore was a lifelong Conservative and a men's style icon. If you ever see me rocking a navy blazer with gold buttons or an elegant statement tie, consider it a tribute. His name was also a naughty instruction, which is pretty fun.

9. GEOFFREY BOYCOTT (born 1940)

Along with fags, booze and winding up our chums on the continent, cricket is my great love. Britain has produced many a legend in the sport, from Len Hutton to Ian Botham (the latter a Brexiteer, I'm happy to say). But Geoffrey Boycott stands head and shoulders above the rest. A proud Yorkshireman – is there any other kind? – Boycs was the finest opening batsman in our nation's history. He played 108 Tests for England between 1964 and 1982, scoring more than 8,700 runs at an average of 47.72. Which, if you follow cricket, is very impressive.

Sir Geoffrey is what is known as a 'character'. His legendary career involved numerous disputes with teammates, opponents and selectors, and he continued to rub people up the wrong way as a commentator. Some have accused him of exhibiting the self-righteous rudeness of a Yorkshire git. Not me, mind you! In later years, he fell prey to cancel culture (or, as the loony left would put it, 'was convicted of domestic abuse'). But no controversy could eclipse the genius he displayed at the batting crease.

Oh, and did I mention he's a fan of mine? Geoffrey supports Reform and sometimes we text – nothing spicy, your honour! He previously backed UKIP, citing 'the way governments of all colours have handed powers to Brussels'. He also expressed enthusiasm for then PM Theresa May, saying, 'She'll be like Margaret Thatcher – she'll be brilliant.' Hey, no one's right 100 per cent of the time…

10. NIGEL FARAGE (born 1964)

At the risk of seeming immodest, it would be strange not to include yours truly. My impact on British politics is best likened to the bloody great rock that did for the dinosaurs. I won't say I'm the man who killed off the Conservative Party, but I certainly gave the Grim Reaper a hand. Even if I never become PM – as unlikely as that sounds – I'm assured a page in the history books. Though I doubt there'll be any history books if I don't become PM. Britain will have collapsed into a multicultural dystopia.

Tuesday 26 August

Exciting news – I've been invited to speak at Magacon, America's leading right-wing political convention. It will take place in Florida over four days this October and anyone who's anyone in the conservative movement will be there. It's a perfect opportunity to connect with the international hard right and meet some potential donors. Ker-ching!

Money aside, I welcome any excuse to visit America – Sam has long been my favourite uncle. If I'm honest, I actually prefer the US to the UK. Everything's bigger and better stateside, where the sun turns one's skin a rich mahogany. If only I'd been born a Yank! I could wear a ten-gallon hat, live in a McMansion and have a name like Saxxon Kibble or Gunt Fudge.

Plus, I have great affection for that mysterious species, the Real American. These are simple, god-fearing folk with big hearts (I believe the scientific term is megalocardia). They don't need a well-funded public broadcaster or healthcare free at the point of use. They just want to drink their Giganti-Gulp High Fructose Slurry and eat their Quadruple Pounder Beef-Style Burger with an assault rifle on the side.

When I become prime minister, I will use the US as a red, white and blueprint. I'm constantly thinking of ways the UK could be further Yankified. With a bit less social democracy and a few more active shooter drills, we too can be a land of the brave. I firmly believe that Britain's future lies with our transatlantic cousins. That's why I was determined to take back our sovereignty from the EU – so we could give it to the US.

Right, I'd better sort out my ESTA. Like Eddie Murphy before me, I'm coming to America! Though not, I hasten to add, as an African immigrant. ICE might have something to say about that…

He's a wonderful fella, the yank,
Whom the world and their mother should thank
For ruling with class
(Plus, kissing his arse
Will net a few grand in the bank).

Saturday 13 September

A hair-raising experience in central London. Having picked up a new umbrella from James Smith & Sons and reluctantly grabbed a salad, I was strolling down Whitehall to reach my

10,000 steps. Lost in reminiscence of England's clean sweep in the Twenty20 series, I failed to notice a crowd coming the other way. Only once I was surrounded did I clock that all of them were white and most of the blokes had shaved heads.

Then it came back to me: there was a march scheduled today, organised by Stephen Yaxley-Lennon, aka Tommy Robinson. In case you're lucky enough not to have heard of him, Tommy is a British nationalist based in Spain. He's also a hooligan and so far right he makes me look like Ken Clarke. I've taken great pains to distance myself from the chap. His brand of 'activism' makes the anti-establishment right seem like a pack of racist lunatics. Plus, he's got an accent.

Now I'd contrived to stumble into his fascist jamboree. All around me were bellowing patriots, holding signs like 'PRO-TEC ARE KIDS' and 'KEEP BENIDORM BRITISH'. The crowd was a sea of Union Jacks and Saint George's crosses (and a lot of Israeli flags, for some reason). A sense of menace filled the air, as did the smell of lager and Lynx Africa. I decided to beat a discreet retreat.

As I tried to slink away, I bumped into a wall-eyed chap chugging Carling. He must have been munching powdered donuts, because his nostrils and upper lip were completely white.

'You 'avin' a go?!' he cried, addressing me in anatomical terms. Then the light of recognition came into his eyes. ''Ang on – you're Nigel Farage. You're a f-ing legend, mate!'

'Glad to hear it. Now, if you'll excuse me—'

The bloke addressed his fellow demonstrators.

'Everybody, look! It's Nigel f-ing Farage!'

Those around us responded by cheering and throwing their lagers in the air. Not wishing to be rude, I gave a sheepish wave. I didn't want to be associated with these yobs, but they seemed strangely keen on me.

'You're all right, you are,' said the man with the sugared face. 'We're on the same team.'

'Ha, well, I'm not sure about that…'

I tried to express, politely but firmly, my intention to leave.

'Nah, nah, nah,' said the energetic donut-fan. 'You should get up and address the crowd!'

Next thing I knew, he was manoeuvring me towards a podium. What the hell would I say with thousands of iPhones pointed at me? I was horrified, but powerless to resist.

Glancing around for something – *anything* – that might save me, I spotted a small group of counter-protestors. Amid the rainbow hair and keffiyehs was a familiar face: my bodyguard Wayne. He stood several feet taller than any of his companions and wore a 'Vote Like a Black Woman' T-shirt.

Seeing me, he vaulted a barricade and bounded forth, knocking aside skinheads like rag dolls.

'Sir, I didn't think *you'd* be here.'

'I don't want to be! I know you're off-duty, but could you possibly help me out?'

The chap who'd been manhandling me – who I now realise was almost certainly on coke – stepped up to Wayne.

'Oi! 'Oo the fu—'

Wayne knocked him out with a single punch. Then he scooped me up and carried me away. It was reminiscent of that film with Kevin Costner and Whitney Houston. Y'know, the one with the bodyguard – can't for the life of me remember what it's called.

As Wayne set me down, a safe distance from the mob, I thanked him profusely.

'That was bloody brave of you.'

'Don't mention it, sir,' came his Estuary-accented reply. 'In the words of Brother Cornel West, "courage is not the absence of fear. It is the working through and overcoming of fear."'

'Well, cheers anyway.'

Wayne returned to his comrades and I decided to make for the nearest pub. Sod the health drive: after what I'd just been through, I needed a Taddy Lager. And very nice it was too! These 13 weeks of sobriety have been a useful experiment but, in the end, I've got to be true to myself. I can rein in my vices, but there's no point throwing the baby out with the bathwater. As my old man – Guy Justus Oscar Farage – used to say, everything in moderation, including moderation.

Tuesday 16 September

Walked past Darryl eating an egg sandwich at his desk. He was watching a video on his phone, sniggering. I enquired as to the source of his merriment.

'It's this Rumble streamer, DrDepraved. He talks about femoid psychology.'

'And what's a femoid when they're at home?'

'You know, females. Women.'

I realised then and there I had to give the lad a talking to. After all, I've become something of a father figure to him. (His actual father's a lecturer in gender studies at the University of Brighton.)

'I'm sorry, Darryl,' I said, 'but this simply isn't on. You can't go around calling women "femoids".'

'Well, a lot of the time, we shorten it to "moids"…'

'No, no, no. It's "lasses" or "fillies". If you don't treat womenfolk with respect, you'll get no rumpy pumpy.'

To my horror, Darryl explained that he wasn't on the look-out for rumpy or pumpy.

'I'm volcel, sir. Practising semen retention to enhance my T levels.'

'Good lord. So you never want a girlfriend?'

'Women won't date me because of my common-sense beliefs about skull shape and miscegenation. Their loss. They can keep having casual sex and catching STIs like Pokemon. I'm waiting for a looksmaxxing tradwife.'

Honestly, I sometimes despair of the young right…

Thursday 2 October

According to Darryl, one of the best ways to generate online engagement is man-on-the-street interviews. Basically, you vox pop people who your followers love to hate, make them look foolish and watch the likes roll in. This afternoon, we hied ourselves to Oxford Street to capture footage of me 'owning' ethnic youths, girls with nose piercings, etc.

We began by shooting my introduction.

'Hi, Nigel Farage here, braving the hellscape that is Sadiq Khan's London. He should really be called "Sadistic Carnage", because that's what he's inflicted on this once-great city. You can't leave the house without being set upon by a diverse version of the droogs from *A Clockwork Orange*. Anyway, I want to find out how much young Brits really know about their history. I'm wearing my stab vest, so here goes...'

Once the intro was done, I recorded the outro.

'And there you have it, folks – complete ignorance of the basics. These kids have no idea what makes Britain great. Why not? Because of our Marxist education system, which needs to be dismantled. Right, better flee this no-go zone before I get bludgeoned. Cheerio!'

All that remained were the interviews themselves. Darryl went off into the crowd to source some victims. Meanwhile, I warily eyed a branch of Five Guys. Aspiring milk-shake-throwers would have no shortage of ammunition.

My first interviewee was a dreadlocked fella in his early twenties, carrying bags from the Nike store.

'Hello young man. What's your name?'

'Marcus.'

'Tell me, Marcus, in what year did Britain beat Germany and end World War II?'

He hesitated a moment. I smiled, anticipating a gormless response.

'I mean, the answer you're looking for is 1945, but it would be more accurate to say Germany was defeated through collective effort on the part of the Allied nations.'

I waved a dismissive hand.

'Okay, fine, the Yanks gave us back-up. But it was our boys who laid down their lives.'

'Actually, the vast majority of Allied military deaths were sustained by the Red Army. The USSR was essential to—'

I cut him off.

'That's communist twaddle, I'm afraid. You don't know what you're on about.'

'Well, I'm doing an MA in European History at Birkbeck…'

At this point, I told Darryl to stop recording.

I hoped we'd been unlucky with Marcus, but all subsequent vox pops proved fruitless. Again and again, the responses were cogent, erudite and incisive. We gave up after an hour.

Honestly, how hard is it to find a woke kid who'll make a dick of themselves?

To call me a racist's unfair :
I'm colourblind, and I don't care
If you're pallid or tan,
Maroon or cyan,
As long as you 'stay over there.

Sunday 19 October

Tomorrow's the day I've been waiting for: my triumphant return to Yankistan. I'll never forget my first jaunt across the pond. The year was 1988 – Ronald Reagan was in the White House and Michael Jackson was in the charts. It was the era of yuppies, shoulder pads and 'greed is good'; of Sylvester Stallone and Arnold Schwarzenegger; of buxom babes with blown-out hairdos and giant, white teeth. In Atlantic City, a young Donald Trump was running a series of casinos into the ground – excellent practice for leading the free world.

Back then, I was a thrusting metals trader – young, dumb and full of commodities. I had travelled from London to New York determined to take a bite out of the Big Apple. I was on the hunt for clients – high-rollers looking to trade on the London Metals Exchange, the premier non-ferrous base metal market in the world. As I emerged from the gates at JFK, I beheld a sea of cowboy-hatted good ol' boys and birds who looked like Marilyn Monroe. In a very real sense, I had come home.

An hour or so later, I was striding through the concrete canyons of NYC, taking in local characters. 'I'm walkin' here!' cried one. 'Whoa, getta loada dis guy!' cried another. 'I work for the mafia!' cried yet another. A classic New York scene. The locals loved me, of course. To them, I was a 'proper Briddish gent' – the Alfred to their collective Batman. Not that Yanks believe in collective anything. Theirs is a land of rugged individualism – and quite right too.

Americans are under the tolerable misapprehension that an English accent signifies high intelligence. Well, who am I to correct them? I soon learned to play up my 'Briddishness' with lucrative results. Over the years, I've snagged many a speaking tour and talking-head gig. I got the full celebrity treatment and even enjoyed the use of PJs (private jets, not pyjamas). Yes, the US has been good to me; unlike their chippy British cousins, Americans applaud success. Plus, I can do interviews half-cut and still be more coherent than 90 per cent of their politicians. God bless the USA!

Monday 20 October

Arrived at Heathrow bright and early with Darryl in tow. He's agreed to come along as my bagman/general dogsbody. A pretty sweet deal, if you ask me. Despite near-terminal Yankification, Darryl's never been to the US. It's nice to help him lose his (figurative) virginity.

I'm not keen on airports – too many foreigners – but they're a necessary evil. Hit the duty free to pick up some Johnnie Walker miniatures and ten packets of Benson & Hedges. It's a travesty that we're no longer allowed to smoke on planes. Doesn't this mean the terrorists have won? Darryl went to WH Smiths and bought a fantasy door-stopper – *An Empire of Dwarves and Flame*, some nonsense like that.

We got on the plane and split up (he's in economy – I'm first class, natch). Between the complimentary champagne and three Johnnie Ws, I'm ready for some shut-eye. See? I'm already using Yank lingo.

Tuesday 21 October

Landed at Orlando International and made Darryl carry my bags to the taxi. I have a suite at the JW Marriott, while he's renting a couch off Airbnb. It was too early for dinner, so I wandered about, breathing in the humid air. Floridians are far warmer than their sullen London counterparts. Everyone you encounter has a smile and a friendly word. This is only somewhat marred by the knowledge that they could, at any point, pull a Glock and blow your head off.

Spent the last couple of hours in my hotel bedroom, flicking between US news channels on a wall-mounted telly. The British media is dominated by lefties: the BBC, the *Guardian*, the *Times*, the *Daily Mail*. We only have GB News – and, to an extent, the *Telegraph* – to give us the unvarnished truth. By contrast, America boasts a rich ecosystem of right-leaning news sources: Fox News, Newsmax, One America News Network, New-Ass News, TruthDump and PatriotFacts. These tell viewers all they need to know about George Soros's International supervillainy and the health benefits of injecting antifreeze.

But as excited as I am about Magacon, I know I must tread carefully. US conservatives are a wild bunch and I can't be seen to co-sign their madder views. Just sensible stuff like climate change being made up.

Wednesday 22 October

Arrived at the John Wilkes Booth Convention Center for the first day of Magacon. It's an overwhelming spectacle. If you came here hoping to be a bit whelmed, you're out of luck! The halls are packed with ladies in star-spangled regalia and fellas in tricorne hats. There's a panoply of panels, from 'The Case for Nuking Canada' to 'Has NASCAR Gone Woke?'. Then there's the dizzying array of merchandise: books, figurines, gun accessories, paintings of prominent Democrats in prison – the list goes on. If you've ever wanted a Newt Gingrich bobblehead or a T-shirt reading 'AOC DOA', these folks have you covered.

Wherever I go, I'm mobbed by hordes of admirers. 'Ohmigod, it's the Brexit guy! Norman! Hey Norman!'* Scary blokes with AR-15s want to pose for pictures. Leathery women throw themselves at me, claiming I sound like James

---

* I've also had a lot of 'Colin's and 'Roger's. And, inexplicably, one 'Fernando'.

Bond. I've heard it rumoured that these conventions are a hotbed of… well, hot beds. Of course, I'm happily partnered with Her Indoors. Even if I weren't, I doubt I'd indulge. As they say, the odds are good but the goods are odd…

The doughty disciples of MAGA
Are known for their libertine swagger.
When throwing a bash,
They go on the lash,
And homeward at daybreak they stagger.

Thursday 23 October

On day two of Magacon, I spent much of my time people watching. The average conventioneer is white, past the age of retirement and possessed of a heroic girth. That last fact is explained, perhaps, by the food on offer, which ranges from carb-heavy slop to the kind of gargantuan steak Fred Flintstone would eat. After a lunch of Free Market Fries and a Budget Responsibility Burger, washed down with Muscular Foreign Policy Soda, I toddled along to the convention centre's 'Crypto Pavilion'.

Now, a lot of guff gets talked about cryptocurrency. Luddites call it 'an obscene waste of energy' with 'an appalling carbon footprint'. Allow me to set the record straight: crypto is not just for money laundering and buying dodgy stuff off the dark web. It's also a great business opportunity. Rug pulls, pump-and-dumps, Ponzi schemes – these are the growth markets of the future.

I'd agreed to participate in a Q&A about a new currency called Pockethole ($PKH). Before a capacity crowd, I enthused for an hour about inflation hedging and the blockchain revolution. I lauded Pockethole's transaction speed, as well as its scalability. I've never used the thing, but this hardly matters to a skilled front man like myself. What's important is that they paid me well (naturally, I insisted on real money).

Maybe I'll launch my own crypto one day – NigeCoin. Its logo could be a frothy pint and it would only be used to buy real ale and British beef.

Friday 24 October

Had lunch with leaders from the evangelical church. Interesting bunch! They may sound like cornfed rubes, but their combined net worth is in the ten digits. On every finger glittered a signet ring, on every wrist a diamond-studded Rolex, and around every neck a vast crucifix made of 24-carat gold. Evangelicals believe in something called the 'prosperity gospel', which states that material wealth is a sign of God's favour. God must love this lot, given how much they rake in from their congregants.

Told the pastor next to me – Garth something-or-other – that, as prime minister, I intend to restore Britain's Christian values. Of course, I could use financial support and his lot certainly seemed flush…

The plump preacher chuckled.

'Our Lord is most munificent. And we are glad to share His largesse, provided the cause is worthy. Tell me, Brother Nigel, are you a god-fearing man?'

'Oh yes – I'm bloody terrified.'

'That is wondrous to hear! We thank the Lord Almighty for bringing you into our midst. Now, in His holy name, would you be so kind as to lead us in a prayer of thanksgiving for the bountiful feast He has bestowed?'

I'm not a member of the God squad, so my grace was fully improvised. I think I got away with it – I just grovelled loads and yelped 'praise Jesus!' at the end of each sentence.

Saturday 25 October

Last day at Magacon. My big speech went marvellously. Of course, the thing was larded with Yank terms like 'deep state', 'DEI' and 'FAFO'. I spoke of the need to defend the West and protect 'Judeo-Christian values' (another way of saying 'non-Muslim'). The crowd lapped it up – standing room only. American rightists have a lot of time for me. They saw Brexit as a dress rehearsal for MAGA's victory later that year. To them, I'm a British Trump, with my own hair and less fake tan.

Returned to the Marriott for a nightcap. American beer is, to quote Monty Python, like making love in a canoe, so I went to town on a bottle of bourbon. Yeehaw!

MAGA
WHITE LIVES MATTER
UCK YOUR FEELINGS
SO PROUD
MAKE GREAT A

Sunday 26 October

Perhaps this trip was going too well, because today the wheels came off. Darryl had booked me an interview with his favourite US pundit: Jonah Tubb, proprietor of a website called BrainBattle. I sat down with the gentleman in the makeshift studio he was using to cover Magacon. A barrel-shaped Texan with a lobster-red face, Tubb cut an alarming figure. Still, I trusted Darryl to match me with people on my wavelength.

The interview started innocently enough.

'Folks, welcome to the show,' blustered Tubb. 'Later on, we'll be talking about chemtrails – too many or not enough? But, first, I've got a guest who pinkos hate almost as much as me. All the way from merry old England, it's Nigel Farage.'

'Pleasure to be here!'

'Nigel, I've been a fan since that Brexit shit. You kicked serious ass. My audience thinks you're a hero for standing up to the global pedo elite.'

I'll admit, his praise lulled me into a false sense of security. As a result, I was wrong-footed when he asked the following:

'In your opinion, what should be done about these frogs?'

'You mean the French?'

'Hell no! I'm talking about gay frogs.'

'Gay?' I asked. 'As in homosexual?'

'Hey, they might be happy too – that's none of my business.'

I pled ignorance of the issue. Tubb explained that an entity called 'Globohomo' was putting endocrine-disrupting chemicals in the water supply, thus changing the sexual behaviour of amphibians.

'And you can be damn sure they won't stop at frogs. If these bastards get their way, soon you, me and every guy we know will be dressing up as Judy Garland.'

'I see…'

From here, he progressed to a series of increasingly deranged conspiracy theories. How concerned was I about the prevalence of Jewish space lasers? Did I agree that the pope manufactured Covid? Or that the bombings of Hiroshima and Nagasaki were a 'false flag'? I found myself on the horns of a dilemma. If I pushed back against the ruddy Southerner, it would alienate potential supporters. If I didn't, I would look like a froth-mouthed maniac.

I managed to stumble through, no doubt resembling a deer in the headlights. Still, I was furious afterwards and took young Darryl to task.

'How many times must I tell you? I don't want to be associated with the lunatic fringe.'

At this rebuke of his beloved Yank, Darryl became defensive.

'Sir, I don't get why you're so worried about *normies*.'

'Normies?' I spluttered. 'In case you haven't noticed, we want normies to vote for us. By definition, the majority of people are normal!'

He looked genuinely baffled. I relented somewhat.

'Darryl, my lad, I think you should spend less time online.'

'You mean touch grass?'

'If you like. Maybe get a girlfriend. Or at least try talking to girls.'

Ambitious, perhaps. But anything that stops him pondering gay frogs is all to the good.

Monday 27 October

Still fuming about yesterday's imbroglio. Darryl contrite in his sweaty, sebaceous way. It's a shame that, despite many high points, my American odyssey ended on a bum note.

Tried reading on the plane (*Churchill's D-Day* by Richard Dannatt and Allen Packwood), but lacked the energy to concentrate. Instead, watched 10-plus episodes of *The Big Bang Theory*, then *Dunkirk*, then *Children of Men*, which I hadn't seen before. It's set in a near-future Britain where the authoritarian government rounds up refugees and sticks them in brutal internment camps. But there's also a downside – no one can have kids. Worth a watch!

Tuesday 18 November

Since I got back from the States, things have gone from bad to worse. Reform is riven by factionalism – backs are constantly bitten and stabbed. On top of which, we keep having to suspend councillors for saying barmy things. Just this morning, Greg told me some kid in Derby was for the chop. Apparently, he'd been sending offensive tweets, or X-es or whatever we're calling them.

I pushed back.

'People are so sensitive these days. How bad are the posts, really?'

Greg showed me the account in question.

'Oof,' I said. 'That'll put hair on your chest.'

'It's never great when someone talks about "*the* Jew"…'

As much as I hate cancel culture, I agreed to the suspension. It's a great mystery why so many of my followers harbour vile views. What about Reform UK appeals to such people? It's not as though we're sending up a racist bat-signal.

Even worse, there's a mole in our midst. Every few days, the *Guardian* runs a story that could only have come from Reform HQ. In the past week, they've reported on my three-pack-a-day Fruit Pastilles habit and preempted a major policy announcement (bring back *Robot Wars*). Alas, our leaker is elusive. Greg seems on the verge of hara-kiri, while Miss Pettycash has set herself up as a sort of witchfinder general, determined to weed out disloyalty.

While I appreciate her devotion, I'm starting to question my own leadership. If I can't control this party, how will I run the country? Then I remind myself that, no, I'm great and all my problems are someone else's fault.

The media want me to lose,
Hence why they distort all my views.
No doubt they will scrutin
—ise linkage to Putin.
That's, as my pal Don says, 'fake news'.

Thursday 27 November

Was woken from a mid-afternoon nap in my office by a series of dull, rhythmic thuds. THUMP! THUMP! THUMP! I traced the sound to my chief of staff's office where Greg was – quite literally – banging his head against the wall.

'Oh God,' I said. 'What's happened now?'

He turned to me, his remaining hair visibly falling out.

'Darryl.'

Greg directed me to his desktop, which showed a video with the heading 'REFORM INCEL FASCIST OUTBURST 🤬'.

'This is all over politics Twitter,' he said. 'Seems Darryl went to a bar in Westminster and tried chatting up some girl. Only it wasn't some girl – it was a journalist from Bravura Media.'

'Those north London Trotskyists? Oh lord…'

'Naturally, she pulled out her phone and recorded the lot.'

He clicked play. Grainy footage showed my head of youth outreach clutching a glass of red wine. He grinned sweatily, oblivious to the camera trained on him. A female voice could be heard offscreen.

'What's it like working for Nigel Farage?'

'Pretty based,' said Darryl. 'I'm kind of his right-hand man. Or should I say "far-right-hand man"?'

Here, he unleashed a dismaying snort of laughter.

'Wow… So if Reform wins, you must be in line for something important.'

'Oh yeah. I'm pretty sure I'll be minister of propaganda. Maybe minister for gaming? We're going to do some epic stuff.'

'Like what?'

'Y'know, make Britain safe for white women like you. Round up undesirables. Deport them, if they're lucky. Forced sterilis—'

I paused the video.

'I've seen enough. Tell Hogg to meet me in my office.'

I gave Darryl the hairdryer treatment. He was a touch defiant.

'You told me I should talk to girls!' he protested. 'I used all the techniques – negging, kino, DHV. It seemed to be going well!'

'Of course it did, you fool! She was stringing you along!'

'That explains why she left after one drink. And gave me a fake number. And wouldn't shake my hand…'

Darryl sighed, chastened.

'I'm sorry, sir. Really I am. I promise not to fall for another honeypot.'

Although the idiot had endangered my whole political project, I still felt bad for him. Who hasn't got carried away talking to a pretty girl?

'Look,' I said, 'you'd better go home for the day.'

Once Darryl had left, Greg came into my office, double-fisting Pepto-Bismol.

'You know we have to sack him, right?'

I said I'd sleep on it.

Friday 28 November

Woke this morning knowing what I had to do. Like Abraham of Bible fame, I needed to sacrifice my son – my gangly, weird-smelling son. Sat in my office most of the morning, prolonging the inevitable. Finally, I donned a figurative executioner's hood and called the lad in.

I had hoped Darryl would realise on his own that his position was untenable and make some peace with it. Instead, he was incredulous.

'Explain what I did that was so wrong.'

'The sentiments expressed in that video do not reflect the values of Reform UK.'

'Which sentiments?'

'Well, er… Those pertaining to… ethnic minorities.'

His eyes, bulgy at the best of times, became bulgier.

'You're sacking me for racism? Sir, that makes no sense. Isn't the whole point of this party to kick black and brown people out of the country?'

'Steady on,' I said. 'There's a line between the legitimate concerns of patriotic Brits and unacceptable bigotry. Explicit racism has no place in this party.'

I thought he might cry, but instead he began to laugh, like The Joker in *The Dark Knight*, or The Joker in *Joker*. Then his eyes flashed with rage.

'I can't believe it,' he said. 'You were my hero. I thought you were the ultimate based sigma chad. Turns out you're just another cuckservative. A RINO – Reform in Name Only!'

I shot him a threatening look.

'Don't say something you can't take back.'

'Oh yeah? How about this? You, Nigel Farage, are *soy*!'

Things descended into a shouting match. I felt compelled to call in Wayne and have him remove Darryl from HQ. It was an ugly scene – tragic in its way. Still, I have no doubt it was a necessary step on my path to Downing Street.

The modern, extreme feminist
Has zero desire to be kissed
She'll shriek and she'll sneer
When you call her 'dear',
Or even so much as exist.

Friday 19 December

You'll have noticed, dear diary, I haven't updated you much lately. That's because, quite frankly, I haven't been in the mood. Things are grim at Reform Towers. Our poll lead has dipped and my attempts to get the party ready for government seem doomed. To make things worse, our former head of youth outreach has been reaching out to youths on a freelance basis. Darryl keeps uploading videos in which he decries me as a liberal, a hypocrite and something called an 'optics cuck'.

Meanwhile, damaging leaks continue to appear in the press. Darryl is the natural suspect, but these stories feature details he couldn't have known, given the timing of his departure. For instance, me failing to declare the gift of a Margaret Dabbs luxury foot spa, which I keep under my desk. Who could the Judas be? Could it be Greg? He always seems on the verge of snapping. Miss Pettycash could easily have been driven mad with sexual jealousy. In my darker moments, I even suspect my driver Iqbal might be some Islamist double agent.

Ah well, Christmas soon. At least I can step away from the tumult and enjoy a break with the family.

Thursday 1 January

It's been a dreary Christmas break, capped by a lacklustre Hootenanny. However, all the turkey-chomping and sherry-swilling gave me a chance to reflect. After weeks of leaks, we need to wrest control of the narrative, to get back on the front foot. To this end, I'm planning a trip to Dover. I'll rent a dinghy, go out to sea and find a boatload of migrants. Boom – viral footage of yours truly shaking my fist at foreign invaders.

Reform supporters will love it. Nothing gives them big feelings like small boats!

Monday 5 January

Back to work at HQ. Everyone loves my idea for a Dover photo op. All that remains is to hire a videographer and secure a boat. Greg suggested an expensive dinghy-rental place. I overruled him, opting for 'Crazy Carl's Seaworthy Vessels'. Reform may have received £9 million from a crypto investor, but we're not made of money.

Friday 16 January

Arrived in Dover for the migrant hunt. I had imagined footage of those iconic cliffs under a clear, blue sky. I would strut about on top of them, gazing reproachfully at the horizon with its concealed horde of foreigners. Instead, the heavens were gun-metal-grey and a vicious wind whipped the sea. Worrywart Greg wanted to cancel the shoot, but I insisted we go ahead. How else would we distract from our various scandals?

Proceeded to the pier with cameraman and skipper in tow. We boarded the dinghy Crazy Carl had provided and set off. Our hope was to find a consignment of military-age males – blokes with big, black beards and sullen, West-hating glares. Women and children would work in a pinch, but they don't get our supporters' blood up like men. To my surprise, though, no migrant boats materialised.

We were out there for four long hours, with nary a Syrian or Sudanese to be seen. Then, before we could make our way back to shore, a squall rolled in. The boat was buffeted with waves – terrifying, really. I can't imagine what it's like to come all the way over from France. Then one particularly huge wave swept in and caused us to capsize.

The icy water knocked the air straight out of my lungs. It took a moment to register that I was, as a hard-boiled detective might say, in the drink. Thankfully I had my life jacket, so was able to avoid Davy Jones' Locker. Still, I was ice-cold, soaking wet and bobbing about like a prick. After a while, the RNLI came to get us (I suppose I should donate at some point).

Like my plane crash on election day 2010, this was a publicity stunt gone life-threateningly wrong. I just hope there weren't paparazzi on the White Cliffs, documenting my misfortune. Coming on top of recent woes, I can't help feeling hard done by. It's like God is punishing me – and for what? Seeking to demonise some of the most desperate people alive? That doesn't seem fair.

Our borders are destined to fall
If Brits don't respond to this call:
I say we pave over
The white cliffs of Dover
And build a five-hundred foot wall.

Monday 19 January

Off work with a diabolical cold. That unscheduled dip in the Channel must have weakened my immune system. I suppose I should be grateful I'm alive, but gratitude's tough when you're hacking up a lung and your nose is gushing like Niagara Falls. I'm taking gallons of Lemsip to get through it – way more than the recommended dose. Screw health and safety!

Tuesday 20 January

It's always tedious when someone describes their dreams, but I must relate one I had last night. While no doubt the product of my fevered brain, its impact was profound.

I was pottering around in the garden when suddenly the skies became overcast. Out of the encroaching gloom stepped a Grim Reaper type, his skeletal finger pointed at yours truly.

'Nigel Farage,' the spectre intoned, 'you will come with me.'

'Who the hell are you?' I shot back, quick-wittedly.

'I am the Ghost of Christmas Future.'

'Shouldn't you have visited on Christmas? That was three weeks ago.'

I had him bang to rights. Nevertheless, he clutched my shoulders with his bony appendages. In an instant, everything went black. When the darkness receded, I was no longer in my garden. Instead of hydrangeas, I was surrounded by burned-out houses, overturned cars and streets strewn with rubbish.

'Where on Earth am I?'

'The not-too-distant future – London, 2031.'

'My God, it looks even worse than in my day. I assume Sadiq's still mayor?'

'Khan has been out of office since 2028. The new mayor is Laurence Fox. He ran on a platform of remigration and forcing Billie Piper to take him back.'

'Crikey. So he's the one who mucked things up?'

'He played his part. But some are guiltier still.'

Looking around, I was confronted with yet more unpleasantness. Tramps warming their hands around a flaming bin. A pair of rats having a knife fight. A group of riot police using batons on a street performer dressed as Austin Powers.

'Oh behave!' cried the poor man, before being knocked unconscious. I gawped in horror.

'There are scenes like this all over Britain,' said my dark companion.

'Who's to blame?'

'The prime minister. He was elected promising change. That he delivered – though not, as you can see, for the better.'

'I can't believe things went to hell so quickly. What did the bastard do?'

'Deported migrants. Slashed welfare. Cracked down on civil liberties.'

I blinked, confused. Those policies didn't sound too bad. In fact, they sounded rather close to my own. Suddenly, a chill ran down my spine.

'Spirit,' I said, 'what is this prime minister's name?'

'You know it,' replied the shade, 'as well as you know your own.'

He pointed again, this time at the digital display on the side of a bus shelter (the only one in the vicinity that hadn't been torched). It showed a newsflash from LBC – my grinning face, beneath the headline 'FARAGE DECLARES WAR ON MAURITIUS'.

'No,' I moaned, 'no, no, no! This isn't what I want at all! Good Spirit, assure me that I yet may change these shadows you have shown me, by an altered life!'

Just then, I woke up.

The clock showed 4.30 a.m., but I couldn't get back to sleep. I rinsed my face, changed my sweat-soaked pyjamas and went downstairs. Having brewed a cuppa, I sat in my armchair, brooding. I'd had a bad dream – that's all. Probably the result of overdoing it on Lemsip. There was no deeper significance, I told myself. Dreams aren't real.

This, as my former colleague Darryl would say, was 'cope'. Dreams may not be real, but they provide us with insights from the subconscious. When your subconscious speaks, it's best to listen. Mine was saying something I had known for a while but had been too afraid to face. It was saying I shouldn't be prime minister.

3.

FARAGE IN CHARGE?

January to February

Friday 23 January

Travelled to Reform HQ to announce my intention to stand down. I kept my own counsel, but Iqbal could tell something was up.

IQBAL: Sir, you're very quiet today. Still feeling poorly?
ME: No, no. Just a little blue, I suppose.
IQBAL: Who could blame you? All these foreigners coming in, threatening our Western way of life. Inshallah you become PM soon, so you can sort everything out.

Imagining his disappointment only made me feel worse.

I had told Greg to convene an emergency meeting. As I headed there, I was intercepted by Miss Pettycash.

'Nigel!' she trilled. 'I have news!'

'Look, I'm a bit busy. Can we—'

She raised her hand to reveal an engagement ring. I was astonished, not least by its size. Who would have thought mousy Miss P was in such demand?

'Well, congratulations!' I said. 'I look forward to meeting the lucky fella.'

'You won't have to wait long – he's popping by now. There he is!'

I turned to see a silver-haired man in his early sixties. He wore a green tweed blazer, mustard yellow corduroys and a Cheshire Cat smile.

'Hello, Sharon!' the bloke boomed.

So that's her name! He handed over some Tupperware in a Waitrose bag.

'Silly me, forgetting lunch,' she giggled. 'Thanks for dropping it off.'

'Any excuse to see you, honeybuns. Plus, I was able to park my Aston round the corner.'

The pair began to canoodle. Then Miss Pettycash – sorry, *Sharon* – remembered I was standing nearby.

'Sorry, Nigel. This is my fiancé, Rupert Lafarge.'

The man gave me a phalange-crushing handshake.

'Nige!' he cried. 'I've heard all about you. Fair play on the politics lark. Couldn't handle that guff myself. I'm in soft commodities – not as exciting, but it pays well.'

I left the lovebirds to their flirting. My secretary seemed happy and I was happy for her. That said, I found the chap rather obnoxious.

With my inner circle gathered in the conference room, I told them my big decision. Greg was so horrified he spat out his Pepto-Bismol.

'Are you mad?' he spluttered. 'Reform's a one-man band. Without you, we're just people who were too weird to be Tories!'

'Sorry, but I no longer believe I'm best placed to lead this country. The British people deserve a prime minister with self-confidence.'

Greg shot me a smouldering look.

'Nigel, since coming to work for you, I've had four stomach ulcers and developed both IBS and GAD. My wife left me for our marriage counsellor. I didn't put up with all that to elect Richard fucking Tice!'

At Greg and the brain-boxes' pleading, I agreed to take a week's holiday to think things over.

Wednesday 28 January

Spent the last few days puttering around the house, at a loose end. I'm used to being the centre of attention. Without it, I'm bored out of my skull. Alas, Her Indoors is out of doors, visiting her native France. Not sure why – baguette meeting, onion convention, something of that nature. The point is, I'm on my tod and starting to climb the walls. Yesterday's highlight was cleaning the bathroom grout.

Made the mistake of checking my work email. Yet another leak in the *Guardian*, this one claiming that I refuse, on principle, to tip Deliveroo drivers. Spent an hour fantasising about what I'd do if I could winkle out our mole. Settled on strangling them with a garrote concealed in my wristwatch, like Red Grant in *From Russia With Love*. This murderous reverie helped pass the time.

Mostly I lie on my sofa, staring up at cracks in the ceiling. I'd say I'm depressed, but I don't believe in mental health. As far as I'm concerned, blokes have two modes: chuffed and cheesed off. Take that, Anthony Clare! Still, I need a change of scene, so I'm going to do something I've never done before – visit Clacton voluntarily. Hey, it can't be worse than being alone with my thoughts.

Thursday 29 January

Arrived in Clacton on the 10:18 from Liverpool Street. People say I only chose this constituency because 73 per cent of its residents voted Leave. Wrong! I feel a strong connection to the area, just as I previously felt strong connections to Eastleigh, Salisbury, Bexhill and Battle, South Thanet, Bromley and Chislehurst, and Buckingham. I love Jaywick Sands, Martello Towers, Moot Hall and all the other landmarks not mentioned on the Wikipedia page. I would spend all my time in Clacton if it weren't for other commitments: parliament, GB News, washing my hair.

From the station, I headed straight to the pier. Had a wonderful time sampling culinary delights, driving dodgems, ten-pin bowling, etc. While I refrained from the more nauseating fairground rides, I admired their airbrush decorations. Where else can one see a wonky Tony Soprano hanging out with Bart Simpson and Iron Man? As I stood on the promenade, gazing out to sea, I could feel my lethargy lift. True, a seagull did nick my pasty. But I was glad to donate a meal to an honest British bird.

Following lunch, I set off on a solo pub crawl. Sank pints at the Bush & Beaver, the Amputee's Arms and the Andrew

Mountbatten-Windsor (formerly the Duke of York). After that, the names got hazy. Everywhere I went, I encountered passionate supporters. These were ordinary Brits, the salt of the earth, people with *Legitimate Concerns*. Unlike most politicians, I actually listened to them. And what they had to say was fascinating:

'Nigel, I despair at the state of the nation.'

'Nigel, you're a hero to us common folk – Britain's only hope.'

'Nigel, we need you to win power and turn our ailing country around.'

Quite a few of them used colourful language about asylum seekers, but that's probably a coincidence. The upshot is that this Clacton jaunt did me a world of good (I'm as surprised as anyone). I went home with a spring in my step and a renewed appreciation for my supporters.

I'll grant you that things have been tough
Since Europe received our rebuff,
But fiscal decline
is no fault of mine:
We just didn't Brexit enough.

Saturday 31 January

Apologies, but I'm going to have to tell you about another dream. After an evening of wine, cheese and soul-searching, I conked out on the couch. Suddenly, the living room door burst open and a tidal wave of blood rushed in. It was like that Stanley Kubrick film – the one about a normal bloke who stays at a hotel with his annoying wife and child. I jumped up on the back of the couch as red liquid filled my living room. Within moments, it had settled about two feet deep. I was surrounded by a sort of blood river – a 'river of blood', if you will.

Then, through the open door, came a canoe. Paddling it was a stern, thin-lipped man in an old-fashioned suit. As he drew near the couch, his heavy brow and blazing eyes were unmistakable.

'Hang on,' I said. 'Are you… Enoch Powell?'

'Indeed I am,' he replied in that clipped Brummie tone. 'Or rather, the ghost of the aforementioned.'

'Good lord. Well, how on earth are you?'

'Not too bad. They have me in the white section of hell. Pleased about that.'

He glanced around my blood-drenched living room.

'Sorry about the river. It's my only means of getting about…'

'Don't worry,' I replied, 'I'm sure it won't stain. In any case, it's an honour to have you here. You're my hero, Mr Powell. I drove you to a UKIP event in '93 – do you remember?'

'How could I forget? I may not have said much on that car journey, but I could tell you were something special. Even from beyond the grave, I have watched your career with great interest.'

A tear came unbidden to my eye.

'Gosh. I… I don't know what to say. What brings you to our mortal realm?'

'You, dear boy. I came to tell you to stay the course. Be the prime minister this country needs.'

'But Enoch, I'm not sure I can. People say I'm extreme, opportunistic, a menace to social cohesion.'

He waved his whip hand dismissively.

'I got plenty of stick back in the day. They called me a racialist, if you can believe it. That's the price of doing anything worthwhile.'

'What if I'm not the right man for the job?'

'All you need is a little grit. Keep buggering on. But not literally!'

I gave a polite laugh. He looked deadly serious.

'I mean "buggering" in the figurative sense.'

'Gotcha,' I said. He pressed on.

'Britain went to the dogs when we legalised that. Nowadays it's all cock rings, masturbation sleeves, prostate massagers designed to hit the P-spot—'

I woke with a start, kicking over a half-full glass of merlot. There were no bloodstains to be seen – just red wine.

I'm writing this in the early hours, unable to get back to sleep. Did I just receive guidance from the other side? Or was it more to do with those nine ounces of camembert?

Sunday 1 February

Awoke this morning a changed man. At least, changed back to how I was. It's as though a great weight has been lifted. I now realise I don't need to be some paragon of virtue, pure in body and soul. I don't need to pussyfoot around offending people or fret about the awesome responsibilities of office. I just need to let Nigel be Nigel.

Does Nigel have rough edges? You bet. I smoke and drink to excess. I make off-colour jokes. I hold views that a plurality of the British public find reprehensible. But such authenticity is why voters love me. If I try to appeal to everyone, I'll appeal to no one. I'm like Marmite, except not in the slightest bit brown.

Right, enough moping around. Tomorrow I return to HQ with a simple message: Nigel's back with a vengeance. Once more unto the breach!

You can't say a damn thing these days
For fear of offending the gays,
Or some blue-haired bloke
Who loves to be woke
And join in this whole gender craze.

Monday 2 February

My inner circle were understandably elated to learn of my decision.

'Boys,' I declared, 'I'm going nowhere. Unless you count No 10!'

There followed much applause and popping of champagne corks. For the first time in about a year and a half, I saw Greg smile.

'You old bastard,' he said. 'I knew you'd come to your senses. Actually, I didn't. I applied for several other jobs. But I'm glad you're back.'

My first order of business is to stop these leaks once and for all. Drawing upon my knowledge of espionage,* I've

---

* *Tinker Tailor Soldier Spy*, rather than Bond.

decided to employ a canary trap (also known as a barium meal test). You give each suspect a slightly different version of a sensitive document and see which version leaks. Time to remove this mole…

Tuesday 3 February

Today I set about trapping my canary. I told everyone in the office their own individual made-up story (for instance, that I have a tattoo of Zayn Malik, or that I'm fluent in Esperanto) and swore them to secrecy. While doing so, it occurred to me that this is precisely how Colleen Rooney caught Rebekah Vardy. Here's hoping my tradecraft proves as effective as Wagatha Christie's!

Monday 9 February

The canary trap worked – Esperanto. I now have the identity of the leaker.

It's ………. Wayne Boyd.

Tuesday 10 February

Having concluded my mole hunt, it was time to tackle Woke Wayne. I called the bodyguard into my office and gave him my best Michael Corleone: 'I know it was you, Wayne. You broke my heart. You broke my heart.'

Confronted with the evidence, the man admitted everything. No tears, no remorse – just a stone-faced stare. I demanded to know how it all started.

'I got talking to a guy at my ethical knitting circle. Turns out he works for the *Guardian*. I told him who I work for and he asked if I'd consider becoming a source. I was happy to oblige.'

'But why?'

He explained that it was nothing personal.

'You're poised to become the most right-wing prime minister in UK history. As a socialist, an anti-racist and a trans ally, I needed to do something. I'll take a milkshake for you, but I can't condone your divisive, xenophobic agenda.'

In recent weeks, his words might have caused sadness or self-doubt. Now, they filled me with righteous indignation. I ordered the man to throw himself out, if that was physically possible.

Wednesday 11 February

Spent last night reflecting on loyalty and betrayal. I confess, Wayne's actions have cut me to the quick. I knew we didn't see eye to eye on politics – the guy makes Zack Polanski look like Jim Davidson – but my life was in his giant hands. Compared to such perfidy, other wrongs seem insignificant.

Perhaps that's why today I went to see Darryl. He's working in some kind of nerd emporium called Forbidden Planet (I knew this because he asked Reform for a reference). I waited beside a display case as a member of staff went downstairs to fetch him. Honestly, who's dropping three hundred quid on a 1/8-scale statue of Deadpool? Darryl appeared, looking paler and sweatier than ever. The lad was clearly mortified.

'M-Mr Farage,' he warbled, 'am I in trouble? Is this about the call-out videos?'

'No, although I'd rather you knocked those on the head. I'm here to say sorry.'

His eyes bulged, Peter Lorre-style.

'I… I don't understand.'

'I was too harsh when I sacked you. Yes, you screwed up. But you're a good kid and you didn't mean any harm – except to the people you want to sterilise.'

I stuck out a hand.

'No hard feelings?'

To my astonishment, he threw his arms around me and sobbed on my shoulder.

'Your forgiveness means the world to me. I promise to stop trolling you on TikTok!'

Needless to say, I was disgusted by this outburst. But also a little moved.

'There, there,' I said, patting his back. 'Stop crying.'

He pulled away, wiping his nose on his sleeve.

'D-does this mean I can come back to Reform HQ?'

'God, no. But perhaps, after the next election, once we have our feet under the table, we can find something for you.'

'That would be ideal. As much as I like arranging trade paperbacks and dusting Boba Fetts, it's not as cool as rebuilding Britain.'

It was a relief to part with Darryl on good terms. He even showed me around the manga section and offered me a free copy of something called *Toilet-Bound Hanako-kun* (I declined). As I made to leave, he blurted out: 'Mr Farage? I'm sorry for calling you a woke-scold NPC. I didn't mean it.'

I smiled at the lad.

'Haven't a clue what you're on about, so no harm done.'

Thursday 19 February

Went on *Question Time* for the thousandth time. Smashed it as always, bringing each and every answer back to immigration. Am particularly proud of my line about fighting small boats on the beaches – major applause. Ash Sarkar looked like she was going to be sick. The robot Labour sent on didn't know whether to call me racist or say my policies don't go far enough.

Expected Iqbal to praise my performance on the drive home. Instead, the fellow kept schtum. After some cajoling on my part, he shared the source of his discontent. Apparently, his friends in the Bengali community are scared Reform will deport legal migrants as well as illegal ones. I assured him that he and his mates have nothing to worry about. Pretty convincing, if I say so myself.

SPEECH UPON ENTERING DOWNING STREET (DATE T.B.C.)

Good afternoon. I have just returned from Buckingham Palace, where I accepted an invitation from His Majesty the King* to form the next government of this great nation.

Or should I say, 'once-great nation'? Because, for a long time, there hasn't been much great about Great Britain. What Shakespeare called 'this sceptred isle' is now septic and vile. One cannot walk down a high street without one's life being threatened in Pashto, Swahili or some language no one's ever heard of. Our schools – formerly the site of wholesome hijinks like raiding the tuck shop – produce wave upon wave of transgender Stalinists. And from Land's End

---

*   Also works for Wills, if Charlie's carked it.

to John o' Groats, hardworking patriots are being forced to take the knee by BLM thugs.

Yes, poor, blighted Blighty is in a bad way. But guess what? That changes today. This election represents a revolution in British politics. They said it would never happen, but an old, white man who went to public school has been elected prime minister. Once I pass through those famous black doors, things are going to be different. I will be a prime minister for every Briton – provided they watch GB News. A prime minister who represents the silent majority that never shut up.

And I won't be alone. I'm bringing some friends with me – renegades from across the political spectrum: Robert 'Ozempic' Jenrick; Suella 'de Vil' Braverman; Nadhim 'Cash Money' Zahawi. These are fresh-faced disruptors, all of whom happen to have been in Rishi Sunak's cabinet. We'll work as a team, taking on the establishment by becoming the establishment. My government will fight every day for average chaps and chapesses, while coincidentally receiving an absolute bomb from billionaires.

There will be those who object to my radical approach. 'Ooh, you can't build that many detention camps!' 'McDonald's shouldn't be in charge of the NHS!' 'It doesn't make sense to ban all pronouns!' These objections will fall on deaf ears, because you, the Great British public, have given me a mandate. The lion has roared and the unicorn has made whatever noise unicorns make. A whinny, I suppose. What that roar-slash-whinny tells me is that people want the old Britain back. Or rather, a new old Britain.

It will be a Britain where you no longer have to apologise for being a straight, white male or having views that some consider 'hateful'. A Britain where the state is slimmed down to the point of anorexia and public services are provided by multinational corporations with names like Palantir, Minas Morgul and Eye of Sauron PLC. A Britain where Boomers can pretend they fought in World War Two, even though that's technically impossible.

Now, there are politicians who peddle false hope, who give simple answers to complex questions, who tell their supporters they can expect nothing but sunlit uplands. I am very much one of those, so let me reel off the following contradictory promises.

I'll boost our economy while deporting hundreds of thousands of workers. I'll help the common man while slashing taxes on the ultra-rich. I'll restore this country's independence while tying us ever closer to MAGA America.

And, in the event that the nation is engulfed by a series of race riots or sterling suffers a Truss-style heart attack, I promise not to take responsibility. My government will crack down on those truly to blame, be they unelected judges or Antifa super-soldiers. At the same time, we will find exciting new minorities to get cross at – Luxembourgers, Chadians, real deep cuts. This will be a golden age of complaining, in which the right holds total power but always plays the victim.

Friends, I am under no illusions about the road ahead. Restoring Britain to her imperial glory won't be easy. However, with a combination of pluck, ingenuity and common sense – all qualities unique to the British – I believe it can be done. That work begins today – right after I've had a celebratory pint.

Wednesday 25 February

Dear diary, I fear we've reached the end of the road. Since my Powell epiphany, I've been a whirling dervish – chairing meetings, drafting policies, and wining and dining donors. Something had to give and that something is you. Diary-keeping has been an interesting experiment, if not an entirely pleasant one. I often found myself talking about my feelings, which is a bit girly. The last thing anyone wants from their prime minister is introspection!

At this project's outset, I intended to provide a record for future historians. Well, the geeks will have to make their own minds up. I believe that actions speak louder than words – and I'm planning some very loud actions indeed. While writing this final diary entry, I was emailed polling data. Reform are still comfortably ahead. As I light a fresh B&H, I picture myself outside No 10, celebrating my victory with a pint and a Churchill cigar, grin toothier than ever.

What will the premiership of Nigel Farage look like? Will it mark a return to traditional British values, and the prosperity and confidence of empire? Or will my hardcore Thatcherism ruin public services, cause civil tensions to explode and wreck the nation's finances? Who knows? And, frankly, who cares? As long as I have a good time, that's all that matters. I didn't think Brexit through – and that turned out fine.

THE END
FOR NOW…

When I become Britain's Prime Minister,
I'll fix all the flaws that diminish her.
I'll start nicking tramps
And setting up camps
For migrants (but nothing too sinister).

BOOK PITCH

To the *Guardian*-reading, quinoa-chomping wokerati at [NAME OF RETAILER],

Sorry to disappoint you, but this isn't Zadie Smith or the bird who wrote *White Fragility*. No, it's Nigel Farage, Brexit bad boy and your future PM. I'm dictating this missive with a pint of Greene King IPA in one hand and a Ginsters pasty in the other. Why? To tell you about my upcoming book, which is called <u>Not</u> *The Secret Diary of Nigel Farage, Aged 61¾*.

Now, I expect you're too cowardly for a title chock-full of British common sense. You'd rather sell a guide to newt preservation or a book containing nothing but pronouns. If that's the case, it's a perfect example of cancel culture. By refusing to order 200,000 copies of my diary, you'll be obliterating the very concept of free speech. Still, on the off-chance you're not paid-up members of the loony left, here's my pitch…

<u>Not</u> *The Secret Diary of Nigel Farage, Aged 61¾* is a rip-roaring account of my everyday life as I prepare for what polls indicate will be a stint in Downing Street. It reveals a side to me that the *hoi polloi* have never seen: running my show on GB News, making money from Cameo and ads for gold bullion, and – very occasionally – representing my constituents in the House of Commons. From romance to political intrigue to terrifying milkshake attacks, this pulse-pounding page-turner has it all.

I'll level with you, [NAME OF RETAILER]: I don't read many books (just Andy McNab and the occasional biography of Churchill). What I do know is how to sell things to the British people. And, I would venture to say, this book is even more appealing than Brexit. We're talking literary prizes, wall-to-wall coverage, millions sold in the first month. I'll be the new JK Rowling – with similar views on trans people.

I look forward to your response. But don't take too long making your mind up. If I don't hear back within

24 hours, I plan to publicly denounce [NAME OF RETAILER]. I'll be forced to use the various platforms at my disposal – X, *Newsnight*, GB News, etc – to explain how my voice has been silenced. It would be a real shame if people started protesting outside your stores…

Yours telling it like it is,
Nigel

PS I also have an idea for a kids' book: *The Small Boat That Could*. It's about an anthropomorphic dinghy that reaches the White Cliffs of Dover, realises the error of his ways and takes a consignment of Afghans back where they belong.

FARAGE ON FASHION

The following was written for a men's periodical,
Modern Cove.

REFORM YOUR WARDROBE
WITH NIGEL 'GLAD RAGS' FARAGE

When it comes to obscuring nakedness, you can't say fairer than clothes. I've always believed that clothes maketh the man (and, indeed, that women cleaneth the clothes). You could even call me something of a dandy. I was a dedicated follower of fashion at Dulwich College, where I used to polish my cadet boots to a fastidious shine and sometimes appeared with cane and snuff box. As a young metals trader, I would strut around the City in a pinstripe suit and brogues. And throughout public life, my clothes have served as a form of party political broadcast.

When I get dressed, I don't throw on any old threads. Each item is selected to send a message: call it sartorial nationalism. You may have seen me decked out in Union Jack shoes, notably while chatting with Murdoch at Evgeny Lebedev's garden party in 2016. My patriotic trotters hailed the dawn of Brexit-era Britain. At other points, I've sported 'Keep Calm and Carry On' cufflinks and a beaded bracelet spelling out 'REFORM'. From fedoras to salmon-pink chinos, my get-up is a joyful assertion of English pride.

I reject the idea that style standards are set in Paris or Milan. As far as I'm concerned, Brits dress better than anyone, the prime example being yours truly. Critics say I'm a fascist, but I'm more a fashionista. In this article, I'll show you how to achieve some classic Farage lewks. It's time to take back control… of your outfits!

1. The Political Fit

In terms of workplace attire, why mess with success? Classic suit, navy or charcoal. Crisp shirt, blue or white. It's a look for ambling through the corridors of power or holding forth in a broadcast studio. A look that says: 'I may have some out-there ideas, but I'm the sort of chap you can trust to run a country.' Dictators don't wear suits from Hackett, do they? They're more into military uniforms and Hugo Boss.

Remember: there's no substitute for a comfortable suit worn with confidence. You don't need some bespoke number from Savile Row – I get mine off the rack. Note that I didn't say 'prêt-à-porter', because I'm not a frog. (Well, my surname suggests Huguenot origins, but we can't hold a man's origins against him.) You should be aiming for something in the £500–£1,000 range, ideally resistant to beer stains and cigarette burns.

While a politician must dress to impress, the awesome responsibilities of office don't preclude fun with one's apparel. When campaigning, I might switch to a tweed sports jacket, checked shirt and jaunty tie (accessorised with a turquoise rosette, naturally). If I feel daring, I'll break out my double-breasted, royal-blue blazer with silver buttons, or that turquoise suit I wore for my conference speech. People listen to me, so I might as well give them something to look at.

2. Fresh off the Farm

Rural areas are fertile ground for Reform, so I often indulge in countryside cosplay. I'm a pioneer of political agri-couture, often seen in a flat cap, checked shirt and tie, with Barbour waxed jacket and mustard-yellow corduroys. It's a look focus-grouped to appeal to Farmer Jim, one that says 'get arf moi land, but only once you've had a chance to admire these pristine wellies'. Call it *Countryfile* chic, or Emmerdalecore.

Now, I'm very much a creature of suburbia – more 'stocks and shares' than 'livestock'. I wouldn't be seen dead mucking out a stable or pleasuring a pig or whatever it is these yokels do. Still, image is everything and this ensemble sets me apart from the metropolitan elite. It's a way to signal rustic authenticity without going full Clarkson. I've even toyed with getting a border collie.

Of course, Britain's countryside contains multitudes. Sometimes you want to look less like a horny-handed tractor-lover and more like a country squire. On such occasions, I either don a gilet or a Covert coat with velvet collar in olive – perfect for beagling, pheasant shooting or the secretive and illegal pastime of squirrel-smashing.

3. Party Animal

All work and no play makes Nigel a dull boy. That's why I keep my social calendar full, mixing one kind of party with another. Farage has it large! And who can blame me? After a long day of shaking hands, nattering on TV and schmoozing tycoons at boozy lunches, one needs to unwind. But how should one dress when letting one's hair down? (Figuratively – I'd never have long hair like some degenerate hippie.)

Well, I'm a fan of summery looks, fit for regattas, yacht-based bonhomie or the *Spectator*'s summer soirée. You might spot me in a Mazzelli pink tweed check jacket with yellow cords, looking like a slice of Battenberg. Or else my blue-and-white-striped linen blazer, as seen at the afore-mentioned Lebedev do. If the function takes place after sun-down – say the New York Young Republican Club Annual Gala – I might favour the crowd with black tie. Who's this debonaire chap? The name's Farage, Nigel Farage!

4. The Junglist

A look I rarely show off, but that's rightly iconic. As a contes-tant on *I'm a Celebrity... Get Me Out of Here!*, I was tasked with surviving the wilds of Dungay, New South Wales. To do so, I equipped myself with plain, functional, hardwearing gear: khaki hat and jacket, red fleece, shorts and socks, and a camouflage bandana. It's garb that screams 'Ant and Dec just made me eat a millipede, but I still feel chic'.

While I'm best known for sophisticated ensembles, some-times rough and ready is the way to go. It certainly gives the

ladies something to think about! At points during the show, I
stripped down to my vest, much like Bruce Willis in *Die Hard* –
not to mention when I displayed my bare buttocks in the shower.
Apparently, the ITV mailroom was flooded with lustful epistles.
I quote: 'I'm a married woman, but Nigel can break my union
any day.' Also: 'I'd get my tits out for Farage – call it Bra-xit.'

Et voilà: four runway-ready Farage aesthetics. Will you, Joe
Bloggs, be able to pull them off with such raffish aplomb?
Obviously not. But you should try nonetheless. As I said at
the start of this article, clothes maketh the man. Britain was
in far better shape when cravats and toppers were the norm
and a chap wore a three-piece suit to visit the privy.

Some suggest my love of finery makes me less relatable.
Rubbish! I may be a man of the people, but that doesn't mean
I'm about to go around in a bin bag or Adidas tracksuit. If you
ever see me in a pair of jeans, declare me an imposter and fire
me out of a cannon. Doubtless the Owen Joneses of the world
would prefer I wore some drab Mao suit. Well, tough luck –
this conservative clotheshorse was born to shine!

EXTRACT FROM SPY NOVEL

LICENCE TO DRINK*

By Nigel Farage

Starring Agent 0.07% BAC

CHAPTER ONE: BREXIT IS FOREVER

Farage, with two pints of Greene King IPA inside him, lit a custom-made Morland cigarette and gazed into the Thames. It was as black and glinting as the Walther PPK he kept holstered beneath a Savile Row jacket. Dark, too, were his thoughts. What the hell did M want with him? Hadn't he just pulled off that job in Clacton? Even the finest agent in the history of the service needed time to relax, watch the cricket and get completely sloshed.

---

* Alternative titles: *Drink and Let Drive*, *The Man with the Gordon's Gin*, *U Only Kip Twice*.

Alas, reflected the handsome secret agent, there was no rest for the wicked. There would always be a new mission: more villains to slay, more luxury cars to drive, more beautiful women to bring to a shuddering climax. Wherever M planned to send him, he hoped they had a decent selection of cask ales. Having smoked his Morland down to the filter, Farage consigned it to the murky depths. He turned and walked, only somewhat tipsy, towards MI6 headquarters.

* * *

Farage swaggered into Miss Moneypenny's office. M's redoubtable secretary glanced up from her desk and shot him a look of thinly veiled lust. She was an older woman (mid-thirties), attractive but for sharp, intelligent eyes. Also, she was white – none of this woke casting you get nowadays. Moneypenny had never done the deed with Farage. Workplace dalliances were, in her view, unprofessional. Still, she was always good for some flirty back-and-forth.

Farage took off his hat and tossed it towards the stand. It missed badly.

'Fuck!' he exclaimed. 'I saw double and picked the wrong one.'

'Hello Nigel,' said the sexy secretary, or 'sexetary'. 'I take it your lunch was of the liquid variety?'

He perched on the edge of her desk, knocking over a pen pot and a framed photo of her mother.

'You know,' he said, belching suggestively, 'pork scratchings washed down with Greene King IPA is a powerful aphrodisiac.'

She leaned forward in her ergonomic chair, giving him a tantalising glimpse of cleavage.

'Perhaps you should spend less time in the pub and more time taking me to dinner.'

'You're welcome to join me at the Gun & Jetpack,' he said. 'Arrive before my fifth pint – unless Q's invented a device that cures brewer's droop.'

The secretary pursed her scarlet lips and raised a playful eyebrow.

'That sort of thing could be considered harassment. Must I report you to MI6 HR?'

'You love it, you old tart,' he quipped.

Moneypenny let out a giggle, equal parts amused and aroused. She could never resist a bit of Farage badinage. One might even call it 'goodinage'.

'Oh Nigel,' she sighed, 'I wonder if your silver tongue has other uses.'

'Sorry, I don't go in for that. Call me old-fashioned, but I think it's gross. That said, I'd be happy for you to su—'

He was cut off by a sharp buzzing. A patrician voice issued from the intercom.

'007,' it said, 'if you're finished with your sexually charged banter, we have a world to save.'

* * *

'Farage...' murmured M, puffing on his pipe. 'A French name, is it not?'

'Originally, sir,' said the dashing spy, lighting a cigarette. 'I believe I'm descended from Huguenot refugees.'

'Surprising, perhaps, given your disdain for our continental cousins.'

'My name may hint at frogishness, but I assure you, I'm as British as a bulldog with bad teeth.'

The MI6 supremo smiled tightly.

'I didn't call you into my office to discuss genealogy. Tell me what you know about Erik Umberto Hellström.'

'Standard Eurocrat,' said Farage. 'Bleeds blue and gold. Italian mother, father's a Swede. We crossed swords once or twice while I was an MEP. He'd be unremarkable if it weren't for the white cat, bald head and enormous facial scar. What does MI6 want with some pen-pusher?'

The older man blew a ruminative ring.

'I grant you Hellström is an unelected member of the elite, straight out of central casting. Precisely the sort of banana-straightener we Brexited to escape. But what if there's more to him than meets the eye?'

Farage gave a look of inquiry.

'SHADE,' said M. 'Supreme Hierarchy for Advancing Devotion to Europe. They're a cell of Brussels-based extremists who never accepted the result of the referendum. We heard whispers about them for years, but nothing concrete.'

At this point, M poured them both a nerve-stiffening shot of Macallan.

'Now, listen closely, because the following information cost one of our agents his life. SHADE has its headquarters in a hollowed-out Belgian volcano. From there, a mysterious leader directs their nefarious activities. Can you guess his name?'

'I'm willing to bet it rhymes with "Smellström".'

'The bastard's planning something big. We believe he aims to use a series of destabilising attacks to devalue every currency except the Euro.'

'To what infernal end?'

'What does any Eurocrat want? To expand the EU to encompass the whole world.'

Farage choked on his whisky.

'But Britain's in the world!'

'Indeed. And once Hellström achieves his goal of global domination, he plans to replace all imperial measurements with the metric system. Instead of pints, you'll be ordering "568 millilitres".'

'My God...'

'We need to know who's funding the bugger. You're being sent to infiltrate the European Central Bank.'

M slid a manila envelope across the desk.

'Inside you'll find a credit card, BA tickets and a passport under the name Chad Thundercock. Your contact in Frankfurt is a girl called Labia Majora. She's Spanish or Mexican or something like that. Quite the looker – if this were a big-budget Hollywood film, she'd be played by Penelope Cruz, Salma Hayek or a younger equivalent.'

Farage sighed and rose, walking to the office's high windows. A hundred feet below, the Thames rolled by, black and glinting. He was in his sixties now, bruised and battered by a remorseless profession. Was he really about to undertake another glamorous, thrilling mission? Could he still plunge into that world of villains, luxury cars and beautiful women?

The patrician voice sounded behind him.

'What do you say, 007? Will you take down Hellström?'

Farage turned to his boss, a cruel smile twisting his lips.

'With pleasure, M. There's a British-made bullet with his name on it.'

If this were a film, the iconic James Bond theme would play here. You can't do that in a novel, so we'll just have to end the chapter.

Spoiler Alert: In their final confrontation, Farage bests Hellström by saying 'regulate this' and dropping 12 tons of British beef on him.

DULWICH COLLEGE
SCHOOL REPORT

Lent Term, 1981   *Pupil: N.P. Farage*

Conduct and Demeanour: Among both pupils and teachers, opinions on Nigel are sharply divided. While some admire his obvious self-belief, others consider him a provocateur and rabble-rouser. It is certainly true that the young man draws attention to himself. In recent months, he has taken to brandishing an old-fashioned cane, wearing a rose in his buttonhole and placing a Union Jack handkerchief in his breast pocket. One teacher caught him with a box of snuff.

This school has seen its fair share of extroverts and we appreciate boys with a sense of humour. Unfortunately, Nigel's jokes tend to be at the expense of those around him, particularly those less able to stand up for themselves. When confronted, Nigel's explanations are incoherent (he claims his accusers are lying, but also says he can't remember, and anyway, it was just playground banter). Moreover, he darkly alludes to some political conspiracy designed to keep him from the role of prefect. His lampooning of Mr Dalrymple's limp may have hastened the poor man's retirement, while his itching powder prank on the 2nd XV was more harrowing than amusing. This behaviour, combined with his fervent smoking habit, suggests a compulsion to push boundaries (and, indeed, his luck).

Academic Progress: Nigel continues to perform indifferently in exams. His contributions to classroom discussion are voluble, though rarely illuminating. For instance, during English Literature, he will speculate coarsely and at length about the sexuality of various poets. He has made it known that he regards the subject of Divinity as 'god-bothering tosh'. He openly resents the compulsory learning of French and insists on using English pronunciation ('croy-sant', 'sill vows plate', etc).

He shows some interest in History, specifically German history from 1933 to 1945. However, he disrupts discussion of such topics as the slave trade and the Bengal famine, accusing Mr Caruthers of 'liberal orthodoxy' or being a 'left-wing do-gooder'. When pressed on the importance of expanding one's mental horizons, he asserts that his mind is just the right width, thank you very much. He sees little point in revising, as he has no plan to attend university (his intention is to – I quote – 'make a bomb in the City').

Extracurricular Activities: It is in this aspect of school life that Nigel demonstrates the most focus and commitment. While playing cricket and golf, he displays a zeal one wishes he could bring to the classroom. He's an enthusiastic member of the college's Combined Cadet Force and spends a disconcertingly long time polishing his boots. He's also a keen practitioner of calisthenics (at least, that's his explanation for marching around school with his right arm extended).

Recommendation: Given his drive and panache, Nigel has the potential to excel in any field he chooses. Whether this is a good or bad thing remains to be seen. It is strongly urged that he read more widely, think more deeply and learn to engage with differing opinions. He should also bear in mind that his theatrics can have real and profound consequences. Otherwise, he may prove as disruptive to wider society as he has to this school.

Miss Alma Martyr

Upper Sixth Tutor